THAT THEY MAY HAVE LIFE

That They
May Have Life

by
D. T. NILES

Chairman of the Youth Department
of the World Council of Churches

Published in Association with
THE STUDENT VOLUNTEER MOVEMENT FOR CHRISTIAN MISSIONS
by
HARPER & BROTHERS · PUBLISHERS
NEW YORK

The scripture quotations in this publication are used by permission of the copyright owners and are from the following versions:

American Standard Revised Bible, copyright 1901 by Thomas Nelson & Sons, 1929 by the International Council of Religious Education

The Revised Standard Version of the New Testament, copyright 1946 by the International Council of Religious Education

The Bible: A New Translation by James Moffatt, copyright 1935 by Harper & Brothers

To

W. A. Visser 't Hooft

It is hard, Don Severino, to walk at God's pace.

IGNAZIO SILONE

CONTENTS

INTRODUCTION

Evangelism is the call of the hour, as it has been the call of every hour when Jesus has been taken seriously. Sometimes world events spell out that call, while at other times the call comes through some person who has been in communion with his God. But at all times, when the call does come, it comes as a challenge and a compulsion.

This book has been written at the request of the American Student Volunteer Movement for Christian Missions, to set out in small compass a discussion of the imperative of the Church's evangelistic task. "Foreign" missions are only a part of this task. As was often said at the Tambaram meeting of the International Missionary Council, "the resources of the whole Church are for the whole world." While there is the distinction administratively between home and foreign missions, theologically there is no such distinction. There is only one Church and that Church fulfills its world mission according to a total strategy.

It is the Ecumenical Movement which, though a child of the Missionary Enterprise, yet sets the perspective for it. This movement calls into question both the "colonial" orientation, where such exists, in the policies of missionary societies, as well as the motives of denominational expansion in the minds of missionary-sending churches. It is only too true that, whereas the sending churches easily jump national boundaries in their thinking about the Church, the members of the younger churches find it easier to jump denominational boundaries. One of the encouraging facts is that missionary policy, the world over, is adjusting itself to the reality of the Ecumenical Movement and the existence of the World Council of Churches.

But this is not a book on missionary policy or on practical questions involved in evangelistic work. It seeks rather to be a statement, however inadequate, of missionary theology. Its objective is to trace the connection between God's work in creation and redemption and God's call to all men, through the Church, to share in His work. The primary reality about the world and human life is that they are the scene of God's working. They exist because God is at work in them and for them. Our part in evangelism is rightly conceived, therefore, only when it is seen to be nothing more nor less than our obedience to His call to follow Him.

"Follow me," Jesus said to his disciples, and they followed him wherever he went and in whatever he did. To follow Jesus is more than to carry out his commands, it means keeping company with him. Our place as evangelists is where he already is at work, and our work as evangelists is to serve him there. He is the Master Builder, we gather the bricks and mix the cement. And, if it is sometimes given to us to lay the bricks ourselves, we must obey his pattern for the building.

"Follow me"—that is the call to evangelism, the call which determines the scope and nature of our missionary task.

No one has followed Jesus even for a little while, without realizing that it is impossible to follow him unless one is willing to follow him both into the big places and the small. He loved the world and came to redeem it, and those who will follow him must be willing to stand for him before kings and governors, courts and councils, where big plans are being made and where, often, action is sought to silence the Christ. But no less important is the willingness to follow him in his concern for the obscure distresses of the least of his brethren. When the Son of Man comes in his glory he will be revealed as the One we ought to have followed and served when he was a stranger within our gates or a beggar at our door. Heroic service and humble kindness, both belong to the disciple of Christ.

There is also another sphere into which the evangelist must follow Jesus, and that is among those of other faiths. Here he finds himself face to face with men who think of Christ as unnecessary because they are unaware of the seriousness of the human predicament. The evangelist finds that his first task with them is to point to the light that is in Christ, until in his light they see where they stand. Dr. A. G. Hogg has stated the evangelistic problem, with regard to the non-Christian, in a striking parable. He says:

A sleepwalker may safely cross a chasm by the narrowest of shaking planks. He is too absorbed in his dream to realize the full threat of the gulf beneath. But let him wake and he will fall. Now in soul and conscience men are prone to be as inappreciative as the sleepwalker of the abysses they think to pass. But when once Christ has stirred them to wakeful perception of the engulfing depths that divide the guilty conscience from trust in God's liberty and readiness to forgive, then by no other bridge than His Cross can they win again to "joy and peace in believing." Where Christ has not yet been spiritually apprehended, there may be other ways than He to the trust in God which enables our Heavenly Father to bestow on a man some measure of communion with Himself. But when Christ succeeds in unveiling for any man the judgment of God on sin, in this very act He cannot help making Himself, for that man, the one and only way. Christ is the only way to God that can remain permanently a thoroughfare.[1]

Deliverance from sleep and from sin, from distress and from loneliness, from injustice and false peace—that is the task in which the Christ is engaged and where the Christian must follow him. "My Father is working still, and I am working .... As thou didst send me into the world, so I have sent them into the world" (John 5:17, 17:18).

[1] *The Christian Message to the Hindu.*

THAT THEY MAY HAVE LIFE

1. The Gospel

EVANGELISM is following Christ. Only they, therefore, who have felt the grip of the Christ will realize what evangelism involves; and only they can know how far-reaching the revolution is which must be effected in those who are evangelized. For to be evangelized means not merely a change of label or of community, but such a cleansing of spirit and a change of direction of soul, that in one more life God's purpose for all is achieved, and through one more life God's will in earth is done.

How evident it is, then, that when we talk about evangelism and our share in it as workers and witnesses, we are talking on the human plane of issues whose ultimate reality is in the Divine realm; and how important it is that these issues should be faced not in the public thoroughfare nor on the public platform but in the secret place of the soul. That this book may be a help in that hidden struggle no less than in the open work is my hope and prayer.

I. JESUS CHRIST IS LORD

Let all the house of Israel therefore know assuredly that God has made him both Lord and Christ, this Jesus whom you crucified. . . . Repent, and be baptized every one of you in the name of Jesus Christ for the forgiveness of your sins; and you shall receive the gift of the Holy Spirit. For the promise is to . . . every one whom the Lord our God calls to Him. ACTS 2: 36-39

The town crier is crying out the news; news essential for everyone to hear, for it concerns them all. He beats his drum as he goes down the street and the people run out to ask him what the news is. This sight, so common still in the lands of the East, gives us the truest picture of the preaching of the first Christians. They called their preaching the Kerygma—the proclamation of a town crier: news every citizen must know, news every citizen must reckon with, news that concerns every citizen and concerns him vitally.

No understanding of Christian evangelism is possible without an appreciation of this nature of the Christian proclamation. It is not an affirmation of ideals which men must test and practice, it is not an explanation of life and its problems about which men may argue and with which in some form they must agree; it is rather the announcement of an event with which men must reckon. "God has made him both Lord and Christ." There is a finality about that pronouncement. It is independent of human opinion and human choice.

Some people prefer coffee, others prefer tea, and still others like cocoa. There is no truth which decides what they ought to drink. They can satisfy their own preferences. I have a photograph of my father. It is of great value to me; it is of no value to others. Its value depends on me. But Jesus is not a preference, not a value; he is truth. The truth about him is independent of human preference. He is Lord, whether men like it or not, whether men accept it or not; and being Lord, he calls men to reckon with him.

Values are subject to human decision, but truth is unalterable. It decides for us. "I, when I am lifted up . . . ," said Jesus, "will draw all men to myself" (John 12:32). I will impel them, I will force them to decide. This compulsion of truth which Jesus exercised is amply illustrated by incidents in his own ministry. They argued about freedom; he met them with the declaration, "So if the Son makes you free, you will be free indeed" (John 8:36). At this point argument stops and the decision is forced as to whether one will accept freedom at the hands of the Son or refuse it. They argued about God and His nature; Jesus met them with the declaration, "I and the Father are one. . . . He who has seen me has seen the Father" (John 10:30, 14:9). There is no room for further argument; one either believes Jesus or does not believe. They argued about the meaning of life; Jesus met them with the declaration, "The words that I have spoken to you are spirit and life" (John 6:63). No more argument is necessary; one is compelled to listen and obey, or to refuse to listen and reject. They argued about sin and human responsibility; Jesus met them in the holiness of his own person. That was the end of the argument. It forced the confession, "Depart from me, for I am a sinful man, O Lord" (Luke 5:8).

"God is love"—that is profoundly true. "God so loved"—that is a truth which demands decision. The first is an idea, the second is an event. The first speaks of God, the second speaks of God and me. God so loved, loved me, that He has done something about it; and now it is for me to give an answer. The Christian messenger is committed to proclaim this event, to bid each man see that God has so loved him that He has done something about it, and to invite each man to respond. Sin is the refusal to meet God at the place where God has come to meet us.

Evangelism stems from a deed of God which has changed the whole context of human living. Something has happened to the very structure of history. "Jesus Christ is Lord." It is not that men must make him Lord, but that he is Lord whether they recognize him as Lord or not—Lord of the President of the United States of America as of the Prime Minister of India, Lord of the British people as of the Chinese. To the question "What shall we do?" Peter replied, "Repent, and be baptized every one of you in the name of Jesus Christ for the forgiveness of your sins; and you shall receive the gift of the Holy Spirit." You must change your allegiance and pledge loyalty to your rightful Lord. You must enter into that territory of life where his Lordship is acknowledged. So will you receive your citizenship rights in his Kingdom and be forgiven the life you have lived as an alien.

How much is involved in the fact that Jesus is Lord, that God has made him both Lord and Christ? Jesus himself gives the answer in a parable. "No one can enter a strong man's house and plunder his goods, unless he first binds the strong man; then indeed he may plunder his house. . . . Now is the judgment of this world, now shall the ruler of this world be cast out" (Mark 3:27, John 12:31). Just before Jesus entered upon his public ministry he was invited by the ruler of this world to come to terms with him (Matt. 4:8-9). But Jesus was not seeking authority for himself; he had come to exercise authority on behalf of those whom the strong man kept in bondage. He had come to do battle, not to make terms.

The Kingdom of God is the sovereignty of God in effective conflict with evil. This sovereignty was exercised on the plane of human history. Evil was contested and defeated. The strong man was bound and his house despoiled. The ruler of this world was cast out. St. Paul speaks of the rulers of this age as "doomed to pass away" (I Cor. 2:6), or, to give a more literal translation, as "having been made unfruitful." The source of their life has been destroyed, cut at the roots. They are like a dragon whose head has received a mortal wound, but whose tail is beating the air in the agony and fury of death.

This language is not fancy; it is the hard realism of fact. Those who came to Jesus in the days of his earthly ministry experienced it. They found that Jesus opened up for them a realm of life in which evil was overcome; and where, while it was still operative, it was within control and within bounds. It bore the mark of death (Rev. 13:3). Dr. James Moffatt translates I Cor. 2:6 as "the dethroned Powers who rule this world." They are dethroned and yet they rule; but, having been dethroned, not only is their ultimate destruction certain but also their present power is circumscribed.

Jesus Christ is Lord, and those who enter into living relationship with him enter into an experience of freedom, and victory in their conflict with evil. They are able also to see the conflict itself in a new perspective. The call of the evangelist is not so much that men should engage in a battle with evil until evil is destroyed, as that they should share in God's victory over evil until evil is exposed. The Gospel is a call to a battle whose final victory is already won.

But is this true? The only way to answer that question is to look at the experience of the Christian in his conflict with evil. The strength of evil lies in its incognito character. The devil's first trick is to make people believe that he does not exist. But let evil be brought out into the light and it wilts. The conflict between good and evil is an agelong conflict, but it never was decisive, for good was always mixed with partial evil, and evil always mixed with partial good. In such a conflict evil is not dealt with at its roots. Jesus, by his perfect goodness, forced evil out into the open. He held to his own ground and made evil come out to meet him, until in the glare of his glory evil stood exposed.

What crucified Jesus? The power of Rome was concerned with the maintenance of peace and order; and Jesus was a disturber of the peace. The Sadducees and the house of the High Priest represented the culture of the day. They were the guardians of local government as well as trustees of the temple cult. Jesus seemed as if he might bring the wrath of Rome upon them. He also had attacked the cult. The Scribes were building up a body of teaching to enable the common people to observe the law. Jesus brushed aside the tradition of the elders and pointed men to a God who is both living and active in events. This was dangerous for ethical living. The Pharisees were religious nationalists, the flag of whose faith was the sabbath. Jesus tore that flag down. The Herodians were the exponents of the policy of *laissez faire;* while the Zealots sought to overthrow the might of Rome, if need be, by force. The Herodians found Jesus too intense for them, the Zealots thought him too obtuse.

Concern for peace and order, enthusiasm for cult and culture, ardor for orthodoxy in religion and nationalism in politics, desire for the liberal way of life, passion for freedom from a foreign yoke—these found Jesus dangerous. So was Jesus crucified by a combine of every form of human good brought under the control of evil.

The dynamism of evil lies in its ability to use the good and to appear as good. The drama of the cross exposed this nature of evil and how it works. At the cross evil stood exposed, its incognito shattered, its power gone, its face unmasked. "Jesus made an open show of them," says St. Paul. "He disarmed the principalities and powers and made a public example of them" (Col. 2:15). Now we are able to walk in the light he shed; and, walking in the light, stumble not.

The Gospel, we said, is a call to a battle that is already won. The evil with which we must contend has already been dealt with. Its strength has been destroyed. It has been made possible for us to fight our battle with sin where it can be worsted, to choose as our battleground the light of the life of Christ. "In him was life, and the life was the light of men. . . . And this is the judgment, that the light has come into the world, and men loved darkness rather than light, because their deeds were evil. For every one who does evil hates the light, and does not come to the light, lest his deeds should be exposed" (John 1:4, 3:19-20).

There is a serious necessity that this Christian experience of victory over sin should be correctly understood. The promise of the Christian life is not that we shall not sin but that our relationship to sin will be a victorious relationship. It is a victorious relationship because the victory is already won. We can recognize evil for what it is.

This means, that the seed of sin which consists in a disobedient will is removed. "No one born of God commits sin; for God's nature abides in him . . ." (I John 3:9). The actual sins that such a person commits will no more be an expression of what that person is. It will be possible to speak of such a person as one who sins, but it will be impossible to speak of him as one that commits sin. Sin is no more his motivation. He is one, rather, that doeth the will of God (I John 2:17).

In the actual conflict with sin this victorious relationship means that, whatever blow sin inflicts, sin is recognized as sin; it is seen in the light of the cross and, therefore, to it there is always opposed a will that is truly repentant. "If we say we have no sin, we deceive ourselves, and the truth is not in us. If we confess our sins, he is faithful and just, and will forgive our sins and cleanse us from all unrighteousness" (I John 1:8-9).

This double experience, first of the birth from above by which we are "loosed from our sins," and secondly of the continued forgiveness that we receive by which we are "cleansed from our sins," results in a growing purity of life which is the hallmark of the child of God. "Beloved, we are God's children now; it does not yet appear what we shall be, but we know that when he appears, we shall be like him, for we shall see him as he is. And every one who thus hopes in him purifies himself as he is pure" (I John 3:2-3).

The missionary task of the Christian is to lead men and women in their contest with sin into this experience of victory which is available to them in Jesus Christ. To persuade them that this victory experience is real will not be easy, for it is known in the midst of a conflict of which there is no cessation. And yet somehow they must be helped to see that here is the inward experience that sustains the outward struggle. We have often led people astray by suggesting that the Christian Gospel is fulfilled in the releasing of moral strength for one who accepts it: we have failed to make them see that what the Gospel offers is immeasurably different and immeasurably more. It offers "Salvation"—safety to the soul in conflict, safety in the victorious love of God which is in Christ Jesus our Lord. As St. Paul so wonderfully expresses it, the cry of the Christian heart is a threefold cry. It is a cry out of a conflict that never ceases. It is a cry arising from a victory which will be manifest. It is a cry speaking of a security that is now present.

Wretched man that I am! Who will deliver me from this body of death? Thanks be to God through Jesus Christ our Lord! . . . For the law of the Spirit of life in Christ Jesus has set me free from the law of sin and death. ROM. 7:24, 8:2

No, in all these things we are more than conquerors through him who loved us. For I am sure that [nothing] in all creation, will be able to separate us from the love of God in Christ Jesus our Lord. ROM. 8:37-38.

The Christian word for the response which such a proclamation demands is faith. Faith is man's response to God's deeds. Faith is to accept what God offers and to live by it. The opposite of faith in the New Testament is relying on works. The contradistinction which is suggested is what we have tried so hard to emphasize, that the Christian proclamation is the proclamation of an event, of an accomplishment by God with the consequent call to men to accept that accomplishment as having been on their behalf. To rely on works is to insist that we must win our own victory rather than share in His, that we must expiate our own sin rather than live by His forgiveness, that we must build our own security rather than accept His salvation. The Gospel brings this kind of religion— this reliance on works—to an end. God has come to men.

There is a word of the Psalmist which is a searching comment on the religious attitude.

> Unless the Eternal builds the house,
>   Workmen build in vain;
> Unless the Eternal guards the town,
>   Sentries are on guard in vain.
> Vain is it to rise early for your work,
>   and keep at work so late,
>   gaining your bread with anxious toil!
> God's gifts come to His loved ones, as they sleep.
>
> Ps. 127: 1-2, Moffatt

In the darkest days of enemy occupation in Norway, an interned bishop is reported to have said, "Victory is being prepared." It was. But faith was needed to see behind and beyond the immediate situation. Faith was needed to grasp the hands of the friends with whom victory lay. Only faith can teach the Christian not to underestimate the adversary, only faith can teach the Christian not to underestimate the victory. "God's gifts come to His loved ones as they sleep."

Jesus Christ is Lord.

II. THIS IS THE VICTORY

For whatever is born of God overcomes the world; and this is the victory that overcomes the world, our faith. Who is it that overcomes the world but he who believes that Jesus is the Son of God? ... God gave us eternal life, and this life is in his Son. He who has the Son has life; he who has not the Son has not life. I JOHN 5:4-12

Evangelism is the proclamation of an event, it is also an invitation to an encounter—an encounter with the risen Christ.

Jesus is crucified, dead and buried, the tomb is sealed and the soldiers are standing guard; Caiaphas and the rest return home, for their task is done. "It is finished," they say, "and the Nazarene will not trouble us any more." No, Caiaphas! it is not finished. The seal is broken, the tomb is empty, and the Christ still walks the earth.

The Jews believed in survival after death. The Pharisees who killed Jesus knew that Jesus would continue to live. Their only concern was to get rid of him from this earth. Jesus alive in Jerusalem meant the upsetting of their plans, the ruining of their ambitions, the challenging of their authority. He must be killed. Let his soul go on living anywhere so long as he himself did not live on earth. But just at this point they met with failure, for Jesus rose again. The resurrection of Jesus does not simply mean that Jesus is alive. It means that Jesus is alive here, on earth, back among men.

The resurrection of Jesus was what made Christianity a separate and a distinct religion. Without it, the teachings and the life of Christ would have remained a part of the history of Judaism. "The company of those who believed were of one heart and soul.... And with great power the apostles gave their testimony to the resurrection of the Lord Jesus . . ." (Acts 4:32-33). On the resurrection depended two things: the truth of the proclamation that Jesus Christ is Lord, and the possibility of knowing him as Lord by meeting him. Only by such an encounter would the Lordship of Christ take on saving meaning for a person.

St. Peter, in his proclamation on the day of Pentecost, speaks out clearly. The tomb of David, he says, "is with us to this day" (Acts 2:29). But the tomb of Christ is empty. We do not go to meet him as a figure of the past, we carry around no relics of him to awaken memory or to stimulate devotion; rather we seek him—the living Christ himself—in the present. Three days after the death of Mahatma Gandhi, at a mass gathering held in India, Srimathi Sarojini Naidu opened her speech with these words: "Master, it is three days since you died. Come back, come back." That is the hungry cry of the human soul, the cry for living companionship: it is a presence we want, not just principles; a teacher, not just teachings.

The proclamation of the Christian evangelist is the proclamation of this Presence. It is an invitation to an encounter where faith can meet the risen Christ. *To live in a world where Christ is risen is to live in a world where Christ is our contemporary:* contemporary, not only in the sense that he is never out of date, but in the sense that he is here. We live contemporaneously with him.

But why is the invitation to meet him an invitation to faith? Because when we do meet him we shall find him just as known and just as unknown, just as easy to accept and just as difficult as his first contemporaries found when they met him on the shores of Galilee or in the temple courts of Jerusalem. When Jesus came to Palestine over nineteen hundred years ago, heralded by prophet and seer, prepared for by prophecy and vision, to a people trained through three thousand years of history to discern the hand of God in the affairs of men—when Jesus, the expected Messiah, actually came, he found so few to believe in him.

Stephen found in the Old Testament conclusive proof that Jesus was the Christ; but many another Rabbi, and even St. Paul himself before his vision at Damascus, found in the same Old Testament conclusive proof that Jesus was not the Christ. The miracles of Jesus and the authority of his teaching were proof to Nicodemus that Jesus was come from God; but to the other Pharisees they were proof that Jesus was come from the devil. To the reasonable Greek, Jesus was folly; to the religious Jew, Jesus was scandal: and the three thousand years of preparation seem to have been no help at all. He was revealed to faith alone.

But when men accepted him, then they found the past luminous with his meaning, and they who allowed him to interpret the past for them found that it pointed to him. As it was then, so it is now, for Christ is revealed to faith alone; as for proof it frustrates the very end that faith is meant to serve.

> So we would rest content
> With a mere probability,
> But probable the chance must lie
> Clear on one side,—lie all in rough,
> So long as there be just enough
> To pin our faith to.[1]

What then are the proofs of the risen Christ, and are there enough to pin our faith to? Yes, enough and more.

The empty tomb, without which the disciples' claim that Christ was risen could have been suppressed in a moment.

The linen grave clothes proclaiming that here no human hand had done violation.

The new-found joy and courage of these disciples who had shut themselves behind closed doors.

The cumulative evidence of the New Testament writers.

The consistency of the character of the risen Christ with that of Jesus of Galilee in respect of his dealings with men.

The concerted witness of Christians down the centuries to fellowship with their risen Lord.

[1] Robert Browning, "Easter Day."

The history of the Church and the witness of this history to the quality of the Church's life.

There we have the evidences, and yet we shall not find these proofs sufficient until we meet the risen Christ ourselves.

That, fundamentally, is what it means to be contemporaneous with Christ. It means that we stand face to face with him today, and that we need as much faith to trust in him now and give him our allegiance as the first disciples needed when they met him by the sea. Then he came as one unknown demanding faith; two thousand years of history have not made that attitude of faith more easy or more difficult.

We cannot expect anything else from Jesus. What he asks for is faith: that complete commitment of oneself, body and soul, time and talent, to him, and therefore he needs must approach us in a way that only faith can discern or understand. To know Jesus preparation is insufficient and proof always falls short of conclusiveness. There is no attempt to coerce men into allegiance either by overwhelming argument or astounding miracle. There is always a sense of reserve and restraint, a suggestion of twelve legions of angels held back. But once the venture is made, and the oath of allegiance is taken, then evidence and proof begin to flood the soul. They come as we journey with him, come as we follow him, come as we near our journey's end: until at last faith becomes sight, and we are lost in amazement that at the beginning we doubted him at all.

But must men follow Jesus? What if they refuse? They must follow him, not simply because he is contemporary, but because he is significant. *To live in a world where Jesus is risen is to live in a world where Jesus is Lord.*

"All things have been delivered to me by my Father," says Jesus (Matt. 11:27): and if that is true we must seek for all things from him. To argue that we do not like it makes no difference; facts have to be reckoned with not argued about. Indeed, the whole atmosphere of any encounter with Jesus is charged, not with argument, but with the necessity of decision.

Apart from Jesus, men argue whether God is love; in his presence men believe it and live by it. Apart from Jesus, men argue about the meaning of life; in his presence they cease arguing and begin to follow. Apart from Jesus, men argue about human responsibility for sin; in his presence they fall down and ask forgiveness. To meet him is to know the truth, the truth that sets men free.

But Jesus is significant not only for truth but also for life. All life's questions find their solution in him. He is life's Lord. To live with him is to live powerfully, to live in him is to live abundantly. For very life's sake we dare not refuse to meet him, for he is life. But Jesus is more even than that: he is the way. And to us that more is significant, for we are concerned not only with abundant life hereafter, but also with abundant life here. We are concerned with schemes of practical reform to make this our present world a better world to live in. For many the claim of Christ that he is the way is the most compelling claim of all. But is he?

Has he a vision of that better world? Yes, he has, and no man has ever conceived a grander ideal than his of the Kingdom of God operative on earth. Has he a method and technique? He has, a method without compulsion or casuistry, the only method which up to date has achieved anything of lasting value. Has he a plan? Yes, he has: first Galilee, then Jerusalem, then Gethsemane and Calvary, and finally Easter Morning.

But what about actual plans for us, the hard details of this campaign to make a better world? Christ's answer to that is simply "first enlist." Does that seem to be an evading of the issue? Nevertheless it is his answer. First enlist, and then you will receive orders. First befriend Me and then you will know My purpose. First follow Me and then you will learn My plans. But Master Christ! How do I know that Thy way leads to that better world? You know because it is My way.

To me that answer is sufficient. And even though doubt often makes it difficult to follow; impatience for quick results makes other programs tempting; and inability to see the relevance to the ultimate goal of the daily tasks he sets me, makes life sometimes seem meaningless; yet I am content to hold to him and to be held by him.

We must meet Jesus, for he is the truth, the life and the way.

And yet, may it not be that since Jesus is risen, the decision to meet him does not really rest with us after all? May it not be that he will decide the question for us, and confront us even though we do not want to or are not yet ready to confront him? What must we expect from the risen Christ?

The truth is surely that it is not a question of expectation at all, but of giving an answer to Christ who confronts us already. He is there, he has been there, he will be there until we answer him with our life. We may delay our answer if we will; but to get rid of him is impossible. That we have tried before. We are in the position of the fugitive in Francis Thompson's *The Hound of Heaven:*

> I fled Him, down the nights and down the days;
> I fled Him, down the arches of the years;
> I fled Him, down the labyrinthine ways
> Of my own mind; and in the mist of tears
> I hid from Him, and under running laughter.
>
> . . . .
>
> But with unhurrying chase,
> And unperturbed pace,
> Deliberate speed, majestic instancy,
> They beat—and a Voice beat
> More instant than the Feet—
> "All things betray thee, who betrayest Me."[2]

To live in a world where Jesus is risen is to live in a world where Jesus is inescapable. But why will he not let us rest? What does he want? What is the full implication of being confronted by Jesus? The Gospels give the answer in the stories of the men and women whom Jesus confronted in Palestine.

[2] Used with permission of Burns, Oates & Washbourne, Ltd.

Let us think first of Nicodemus, that ruler of the Jews who comes to Jesus by night; think of what he says to Jesus, of all that he grants, of all that he accepts. I accept, he says, that you are a Rabbi. I accept that you are a greater Rabbi than I. I accept that you are from God, and that God is with you. Jesus looks at him and says, "Nicodemus, you must be born again." That was the one thing which Nicodemus did not expect, the one thing he would not accept. He had hoped to make a natural transition from where he stood to where Jesus was, and to begin all over again was the one thing he would not do.

Or think again of that rich man who comes to Jesus. I accept you, he says, as a teacher. I accept you as a good teacher; and if by calling you good there is the implication that I have called you God, I accept even that. What must I do to inherit eternal life? Jesus says to him, "Sell what you possess and give it to the poor . . . and come, and follow me" (Matt. 19:21). That was the one thing he did not expect, the one thing he would not accept.

Or think again of the woman at the well, the woman of Samaria. I accept you, she says, as a Rabbi. I accept you as a prophet. I accept that you can pronounce on the vexed question between the Jew and the Samaritan as to the place of worship. Must we worship in Jerusaleum or is it enough to worship on Mount Gerizim? Jesus looks at her and says, "Go, call your husband." That was the one thing she did not expect, the one thing she had to accept.

That is what it means to be confronted by Jesus. It means that he stretches his hand over those areas of our life which are not yet under his control, and that he seeks dominion there.

We all know the figure of the risen Christ knocking at the Soul's closed door; but let us not forget, as we are apt to forget, that the knock persists as long as any door remains closed. In the lives of most of us, the garden gate is open, so Jesus is not knocking there. The hall door is open and Jesus is not knocking there either. It is perhaps the bedroom door that is closed and that is where Jesus is knocking, or perhaps it is the door of the study—the room where we dream our ambitions and plan our future. We know each one for himself and herself just where the Master is knocking, and we know too just why we have not yet opened to him.

But let us remember this, that while we can refuse to open, while we can reject his claim, there is one thing we cannot do, and that is get rid of him. He remains the inescapable Christ. Knocking, knocking, knocking, persistently and patiently knocking, he besieges our soul until every door is opened and every area of life is handed over to his control.

One thing more needs to be said about this experience, that though Jesus knocks and knocks patiently, he only waits until the key is turned, and then he forces entrance. What I mean is, that while for a time we can refuse to heed that knock, it ultimately begins to get on our nerves, until in sheer despair and unable to resist any longer we turn the key. If Jesus waited until we threw the door wide open, perhaps he would wait in vain, for we may lock the door again. What he does in his abounding grace is to push the door wide open once the key is turned, enter in and assume control.

His parable of himself as a thief who enters the house, binds the owner and takes possession, is a parable illustrating also his entry into our lives. What a terrible experience! Yes, it is. It is terrible to fall into the hands of the living God, but it is terrible only till we fall.

Jesus asks for full possession. Can he have it? Will we allow it? We must. In the light of Christ it is demanded by the sheer urgency of the world's situation, by our own predicament and by the very tasks that await us.

There are tasks to be accomplished, deeds to be done, wrongs to be righted and souls to be saved. Christ wants men. *To live in a world where Jesus is risen is to live in a world where Jesus is at work.*

2. *The World*

EVANGELISM is the proclamation of an event and an invitation to an encounter. This was our definition, and in terms of it, we have sought to understand both the significance of the event as well as the nature of the encounter. It is unnecessary to emphasize that one becomes an evangelist only as this event and this encounter become the determining realities of one's own Christian experience. Evangelism is not a program, it is being a Christian. "He who has the Son has life."

We, now, turn to a consideration of the world to which the Evangel comes. A theology of evangelism must necessarily take into account the inwardness of human life, the situation to which the Evangel is addressed. In order to do this, we shall take the temptations of Jesus as the material of our basic study, for it is there that we can find a true assessment of the nature of human need. And then we shall proceed to a study of the way in which Jesus faced the task of his own ministry.

I. IF YOU ARE THE SON

And he fasted forty days and forty nights, and afterward he was hungry. And the tempter came and said to him, "If you are the Son of God...." Then Jesus said to him, "... You shall not tempt the Lord your God." Again, the devil ... said to him, "... If you will fall down and worship me." Then Jesus said to him, "... You shall worship the Lord your God and him only shall you serve."

MATT. 4:2-10

"Thou art my beloved Son"—these words constituted the mission of Jesus (Mark 1:11). His was the task of being the Son.

33

Prophets had been called by God and entrusted with a message to deliver, leaders had been raised by God and entrusted with a work to perform; and in the case of all these their message and their work were greater than they. But in the case of Jesus, he himself was the message; his commission was to be the Son. He is called to embody a fact, not simply to perform a work.

Basic to every problem of man is the nature of man himself: and it is in this area of man's thought about himself that sin has built its citadel. Let a man know himself as he truly is and the citadel is captured, the fight with sin henceforth is only on the outskirts of the soul. Forty days earlier it had been declared, "Thou art my beloved Son." Now forty days later the question is asked, "If thou art the Son?" Is it not necessary to make sure of one's sonship by putting it to the test and finding out whether it works? Or, if one is sure, what is the use of that sonship unless one can utilize it when one is hungry? Use it, prove it, get God to act on your behalf. Jesus said No. God has spoken and that is enough. This world is not My home, bread is not My food, man lives by God's word.

So Jesus lived. Hungry or satisfied, rejected or accepted, amidst the plaudit of the crowd or alone, he showed himself the Son of God. The devil "departed from him until an opportune time," the Gospel says (Luke 4:13). And that time came when Jesus was hanging on the cross, "If you are the Son of God," said the devil, "come down. . . ." (Matt. 27:40). "Then Jesus, crying with a loud voice, said, 'Father, into thy hands I commit my spirit!'" (Luke 23:46).

The primary fact of human existence to which the Gospel is addressed is man's lack of faith in his essential dignity, his willingness to be and his satisfaction in being part of the crowd, a cog in a machine, a unit in a mass. As many people have been converted to Christianity, it has been said, by a proclamation of Genesis 1:1 as by a proclamation of John 3:16; by the proclamation of God as Creator as by the proclamation of God as Redeemer. In the Gospel, both these belong together, for the Gospel is God's address to man telling him that he is created being and claiming him as son. He who has heard and responded to the Gospel has been through that experience in which he stood distinguished from his fellows and alone with God, where he counted for one, where God called him by his name and claimed him as His own.

A minister was visiting a member of his congregation. There were many children in the home. The minister asked the mother, "How many children have you?" The mother began to count on her fingers, "John, Lucy, Mary—" when the minister interrupted, "I don't want their names, I asked for their number." The mother replied indignantly, "They have names not numbers." How true. How true about God and us. "I have called thee by thy name," He says, "thou art mine" (Is. 43:1). Are not two sparrows sold for a farthing, but if you spend two farthings, do you not get four sparrows and one extra? Truly, said Jesus, even that one sparrow which is of no value to the vendor does not fall without your Father's knowledge. Are you not of much more value than many sparrows? (Matt. 10:29, Luke 12:6.) "If you are the Son of God?"—there is no "if"—we are.

To those who have been established by the Gospel in this sonship, the Gospel remains thereafter the Word by which they live. It is their one safety against an anonymous existence, their one answer to the tempter in the dreary hours of monotony and routine when the wilderness becomes oppressive, their one hope when the hour of exaltation has passed and the elemental needs of life are felt. This world is not a world of men, but a world for them, wherefore the primary need is that man himself should be rescued and vested with his true dignity.

> What is man that thou art mindful of him,
> or the son of man, that thou carest for him?
> Thou didst make him for a little while lower than the angels,
> thou hast crowned him with glory and honor,
> putting everything in subjection under his feet. . . .
>
> As it is, we do not yet see everything in subjection to him.
> But we see Jesus . . . crowned with glory and honor

> because of the suffering of death. . . . For it was fitting
> that he . . . in bringing many sons to glory, should make
> the pioneer of their salvation perfect through suffering.
> HEB. 2:5-11

Jesus is the Son, and he is not ashamed to call us brethren.

But Man is only one capital letter of the human situation to which the Gospel is addressed. The other capital letter is Life. Man must live. The prophet Isaiah so understood the poignancy of man's struggle for food that he described the day of the Lord in terms of a great banquet. "On this hill of Sion for all nations the Lord of hosts will spread a banquet of rich food . . . ; and on this mountain shall he strip away the mourning shroud from all mankind" (Is. 25:6-7, Moffatt).

The Messianic banquet—that was the temptation for Jesus, and it was a temptation not because bread was not relevant to life but because it was. We cannot live without bread, and the result is that we come to think that to live by bread is Life. The Gospel sets the search for bread in a new perspective and thereby determines the form that search shall take. "But seek first his kingdom and his righteousness, and all these things shall be yours as well" (Matt. 6:33). "For what does it profit a man, to gain the whole world and forfeit his life" (Mark 8:36). If the rule of God, and that which it is right to do under that rule, become the determining facts in human living, then food will cease to be a struggle. It will be added. Until then, however, in order to meet the problem of food for the hungry, even while men are being challenged to accept the obligations of the Kingdom, courses of action will be necessary that give immediate results. And yet, if any course of action is adopted which militates against acceptance by men of the righteousness of the Kingdom, then food shall have been provided at the expense of Life. The Gospel underlines the need for bread, and then puts a question mark against it. "Man shall not live by bread alone."

"My food," said Jesus, "is to do the will of him who sent me" (John 4:34). That is what is truly sustaining. To live is not enough; one must have Life: and bread should be not merely the means of living but a sacrament of Life. In order to answer the tempter, Jesus went back to the time when in the wilderness Israel hungered and God gave them manna. "He humbled thee, and suffered thee to hunger, and fed thee with manna . . . ; that he might make thee know that man doth not live by bread only, but by everything that proceedeth out of the mouth of the Lord doth man live" (Deut. 8:3). Manna is true bread, all bread must be seen as manna. It is not enough to eat of the loaves, it is necessary to see them as signs (John 6:26), pointing to the bread that truly sustains, the bread of Life.

When Israel hungered in the wilderness the people desired to go back to Egypt. In Egypt there was food, even though it was food without freedom. But God forbade them to go back. Life in Egypt was not life, it was death; a death more terrible than actual death in the wilderness. For in the wilderness man was still on the way to the promised land.

The Gospel, addressed to man struggling with the problems of living, comes to him speaking of Life. It gives importance to man's struggle, it also makes that struggle secondary. The Bread of Life is already given, it says, and this is free, available now. "He who comes to me shall not hunger, and he who believes in me shall never thirst" (John 6:35). Therefore, man's unconscious assumption that Life is significant in itself is denied, bread is invested with meaning as subserving the true purpose of Life, and the struggle for bread is divested of its ability to breed bitterness. It is a fact that religion is an opiate of the masses: for true religion does put to sleep the urge for revenge.

Another basic reality in the human situation to which the Gospel is addressed is man's attitude to his own endeavor. The Gospel meets the human situation with respect to man's attitude to himself and establishes him in his faith as a son of God. The Gospel meets the human situation with respect to man's attitude to his needs and brings to him a profound satisfaction to condition all his striving. The Gospel meets the human situation with respect to man's attitude to his own endeavor and delivers him from his tragic bondage to results.

The tempter said to Jesus, "All the kingdoms of the world and the glory of them are mine; worship before me and it shall all be thine." Jesus answered, "Only God is of ultimate worth, Him shalt thou worship and Him only shalt thou serve." It is a serious temptation to treat the goals we pursue as of ultimate worth, to sacrifice everything to attain them, to forget that nothing is worth achieving which, when we have achieved it, cannot be offered to God in worship. Peter and Judas were both disciples of Christ. Peter worshiped Jesus and followed him, Judas followed him because he worshiped the ideal of the Kingdom of God; a Kingdom, as he understood it, of freedom for Israel. Peter followed Jesus in spite of disappointment, Judas betrayed him.

At the close of the Amsterdam Assembly of the World Council of Churches in 1948, its general secretary made this statement: "We must make sure that we do not decide that we shall succeed. If we decide to succeed then we may succeed without succeeding in God's way. But if we go on from day to day seeking to do His will, then we shall be prepared to receive success from Him if He wills it; and if He does not, then humbly to say—It is God's decision that David shall not build the temple, but He will raise up Solomon."

Obedience is ours to render, success is His to command. Ultimately, it is not a question of what we achieve but whom we worship. The devil appealed to the words of prophecy which spoke of the setting up of the Davidic Kingdom when the Messiah came (Is. 9:6); Jesus replied by setting that prophecy in the context of man's true relation to God. "When Jehovah shall bring thee into the land which he sware unto thy fathers . . . to give thee, great and goodly cities, which thou buildest not, and houses full of all good things, which thou filledst not, and cisterns hewn out, which thou hewedst not, vineyards and olive-trees, which thou plantedst not, and thou shalt eat and be full; then beware lest thou forget Jehovah. . . . Thou shalt fear Jehovah; and him shalt thou serve. . ." (Deut. 6:10-13).

At a time such as ours when so much human effort is bent toward the achievement of the Parliament of man, these words of Scripture to which Jesus refers are of special value. They bring to us the warning against making "success" the criterion of the paths we pursue and the methods we employ. He who worships the kingdoms of this world does find it easier, for a time, to make them his possession—but what then? We need to remember that, when we arrive at the land of our dreams, our inheritance will be what God Himself has accomplished.

There are four world currents in our time.

There are the attempts to make life meaningful apart from God. Existentialism is only the best known of these attempts. The Gospel answers that true meaning lies in the fact that we are sons of God.

There are the attempts to direct man's struggle for food away from man's hunger for God. Communism is only the best known of these attempts. The Gospel answers, living is not Life, for Life is to live with God.

There are the attempts to erect a human society that will not commit suicide, to balance mutual self-interest so that mankind is safe. These attempts together make up "Internationalism" in all its forms. The Gospel presents Internationalism with its ultimate critique. What is the end of man?

And then finally there are the attempts to salvage world peace through a revival of religion. "Religionism," we may call this phenomenon. At the heart of it is the temptation to use God for human ends.

"You said you live by God's word," said the tempter; "here it is. He will give His angels charge of you to guard you, and on their hands they will bear you up. Jump down. Use this promise of God, and men will follow you into your Kingdom. They are expecting

the Son of Man to come with the clouds of heaven" (Dan. 7: 13).
Jesus answered, It is also written, thou shalt not prove the Lord
thy God. Thou shalt not say as they said at Massah, when they
proved Him—Is the Lord among us or not? (Deut. 6: 16.) The
address of religion must be to faith. There can be adduced no overwhelming argument, there can be wrought no astounding miracle,
that will stampede men into an acceptance of God. Where religion
is used directly to accomplish any other end except to arouse the
obedience of faith it becomes a betrayal of God. God is not meant
for use.

The Gospel takes human life and invests it with divine dignity.
It takes human need and sheds on it the light of the divine purpose.
It takes human endeavor and sets it free from the tyranny of results. It takes human faith and attaches it to God. Evangelism is to
work unto this end.

II. THAT THEY MAY HAVE LIFE

I am the door; if any one enters by me, he will be saved, and will
go in and out and find pasture. The thief comes only to steal and kill
and destroy; I came that they may have life, and have it abundantly.
I am the good shepherd. The good shepherd lays down his life for his
sheep. . . . And I have other sheep, that are not of this fold; I must
bring them also, and they will heed my voice. JOHN 10:9-16

Life is a whole and must be treated as a whole. Any attempt to
departmentalize it must end in disaster, for life itself will wreck
such an attempt. Indeed it has already done so, and we are living
amidst the ruin we have achieved by enthroning different gods for
different areas of life. One good for the employer and another good
for the employee, one right for the big powers and another right
for the small powers, one standard for the white races and another
standard for the colored, one code for Sundays and another for
weekdays, one logic for others and another logic for oneself . . .
the whole thing has collapsed.

What the world needs is a God who will take life as a whole, treat it as a whole and direct it as a whole; a God who is equally interested in the good of all men and nations and peoples; a God to whose economy nothing that makes up life is irrelevant and for whose guidance no human problem is trivial. He must be a God vitally interested in man as man.

But even that is not enough. He must also be a God from the other side. No god who is man-made can be adequate for man. For it is man's smallness and selfishness and sinfulness that have produced and accentuated the ills of our world, and there can be no solution from a god who himself partakes of man's stature, as he must, if man has created him. God, to be God to men in very truth, must have the power and purpose to remake men—body, mind and spirit.

What do we mean by man-made gods? We mean simply that the effectual gods in the lives of many people are gods which they themselves have made. A man's god is the person or thing which controls him. He or it controls him by being the final authority for his thought, the standard which regulates his conduct, the foundation on which his life is based and the value which determines his life's direction. The labeling of men and women according to the religions they profess, which is practically always one of the recognized religions of the world, is often misleading. The true name of a person's god is that of the person or thing which possesses him.

In the case of some, their god is one person or thing. Thus, some men are controlled by a desire for wealth. If any action will bring them more wealth, that action is right. It is wealth they live for, and for it they toil. It is their god. But not all are unified to the extent that their lives are completely dedicated to one single, simple god. For unification is costly, and not all are willing to pay the price. The majority live in compartments, each area of life's interests being controlled by a different god. And the gods of these various compartments are more or less related to one another in an ideological system, the relationship being established through a controlling idea. Thus there are many whose life's ground plan can be fairly described as, "Business is business, religion is religion, sex is sex, and that which ultimately counts is success."

In such a system the various gods will not all be consistent one with the other, for they can be and are derived from almost anywhere. And yet precisely because of this possibility of inconsistency, such a system serves as an ideal god, since it does not demand the price of complete integration; while at the same time, it offers the experience of a partial or false integration. In other words, it is just the kind of god which men can worship and satisfy, while at the same time, they can do as they like.

But not all live thus compartmentally. There are many whose lives are dedicated to one single, simple ideal. Their god is a totalitarian god. Yet, here too, there is often present a great difficulty, for unless this all-controlling god is big enough it cannot offer guidance to men in all their interests; the result being either that men's lives shrink to the size of their god or other gods take charge of the outside areas. Even when the god is big enough there remains the more ultimate question as to whether the god is true. For "if then the light in you is darkness, how great is the darkness!" (Matt. 6: 23).

It is in this situation, of competing gods and of men searching for God, of dethroned gods and of men fleeing from God, of fragmental life and of men seeking wholeness, that the Gospel of God in Christ has to be proclaimed. A solemn fact of this situation is also an unwillingness on the part of so many to commit their lives to God, while there is at the same time such a willingness to dedicate their lives to causes which, while good in themselves, make ultimate claims on men, claims which only God can make.

It seems to be true today, in a more tragic sense than perhaps it was true in the past, that men are not merely prodigal from their Father's home but have actually forgotten its whereabouts. Some seem to have forgotten even that they have a Father. Christ came to announce the fact of the Father, to reveal the Father's love and to be the Father's saving grace to men. He came to us in the far country. He paid the price of seeking us out there. He found us and shamed us out of our sin. He assured us of our Father's love and welcome. He led us home.

To us whose experience this is, belongs the privilege and responsibility of announcing the fact and the act of God in Christ. It is our task to make the Father's address known, to be signposts directing travelers to the Father's presence, to be guides showing the way to the Father's home.

How can we accomplish this task? How can we help men to see that Jesus is the true Shepherd of their lives, and that it is through him they can enter into life's fullness? How can we help them to make the Christ-God discovery?

They cannot begin with God, since to ask for God is to ask for the unknown: and yet they do begin with God since this search for God is the cry of the soul for home, and that cry is man's starting point. Men do not know whom they are looking for but, when they find Him, they will be able to recognize Him. That is the paradox of the religious search, and it is as Jesus fulfills this paradox that men know that he is God.

God is the ground of being, so that it is meaningless to speak about proving the existence of God. It is not possible to get outside God in such a way as to make Him an object of proof. What is possible and what is necessary is to come to rest consciously in Him. The "anxiety" which haunts the human spirit is the best security against its coming to rest anywhere except in God. "Our souls are restless until they rest in Him."

What, then, are the questions to which we shall address ourselves as we seek to set forward the significance of Jesus?

First of all, the question as to the way in which he handles life: Is there wholeness in his method?

And, secondly, the question as to the nature of his relationship to men: Does he meet them as Lord or Leader?

His wholeness of Method:

1. Jesus viewed life as a whole and treated it as a whole.

The way in which he met his temptations shows how he refused to adopt any method in his work which would mean winning the allegiance of only part of the individual. He would neither appeal through the satisfaction of bodily wants, nor would he work by compromise, nor achieve his end by stampeding men into allegiance by emotional assault. He would use only that method which would succeed in winning for God the complete loyalty of the whole man. (Luke 4:3-12.)

Jesus' Kingdom-concept was all-inclusive. The Kingdom was meant for all, and the only qualification for entrance into the Kingdom was obedience to the will of the King. This obedience, which was the principle of integration for the individual, was also the regulative principle in the relation of individuals to one another. The method of Jesus with individuals fulfilled in them the very qualities which Jesus expected of them as citizens of the Kingdom. (Matt. 7:21, 12:50.) Truly did Jesus say that he came that men might have life and have it to the full, and have it whole. (Luke 19: 9-10.)

2. Jesus was equally concerned for all, and in the good of all.

We see how he broke down every single barrier that existed in his day between man and man, and interest and interest. He enlisted Simon the Zealot as a disciple, setting aside political distinction. (Luke 6.15.) He dined with Zacchaeus, setting aside class distinction. (Luke 19: 5.) He conversed with the woman of Samaria, setting aside sex distinction. (John 4:27.) He responded to the appeal of the Syrophoenician woman, setting aside race distinction. (Mark 7:26.) He extolled the faith of the Centurion, setting aside national distinction. (Matt. 8:10.) He befriended sinners, setting aside popular distinction. (Matt. 11:19.) He allowed the woman who was a sinner to touch him, setting aside reputational distinction. (Luke 7:39.) He praised the poor widow who gave her mite, setting aside economic distinction. (Mark 12:43.) He washed his disciples' feet, setting aside the master-servant distinction. (John 13:14.) He rebuked his disciples for their intolerance toward that follower who was not of the twelve, setting aside denominational distinction. (Mark 9:39.) He enjoyed the company of children, setting aside age distinction. (Mark 21:15.) His was a barrierless love.

The interest of Jesus in the good of all was seen also in this, that he never lowered his standards in the case of anybody, however important they were, and however much their discipleship would have meant added reputation for his cause. He was interested in them and not himself. To Nicodemus, politically great, he said: You must begin all over again. You must be born anew. (John 3:3.) To the Scribe, ecclesiastically great, he said: Follow me, if you will, but you will have nowhere to lay your head. (Matt. 8: 20.) To the rich man, economically great, he said: Your riches are your hindrance, give them to the poor. (Luke 18:22.) To Simon the Pharisee, socially great, he said: You love little for only in a little way have you sought or received forgiveness. (Luke 7:47.) His was a love without dissimulation.

3. Jesus reckoned with man as he was.

During the last war, a Belgian student who was a member of a Bible-study group wrote as follows to a friend: "We are hungry most of the time and with little to do: but we have formed a group for studying the Bible. It is the only Book which does not tell lies about man."

According to Jesus, man needs a change of direction of soul. As he is, he is facing in the wrong direction. (Mark 1:15.)

According to Jesus, man needs the discipline of a dominant desire. As he is, the various parts of him obey their own impulses. (Matt. 18:8, 9.)

According to Jesus, man needs integration. As he is, he is a divided personality. (Matt. 6:22-24.)

According to Jesus, man needs stability. As he is, he is a creature of his circumstances. (Mark 4: 15-19.)

According to Jesus, man needs a renewal of his whole personality. As he is, his life is partial and warped. (John 3: 3-6.)

According to Jesus, man needs health. As he is, he is ill. (Mark 2: 17.)

According to Jesus, man needs a revelation of God from God. As he is, he does not and cannot know the Father. (Matt. 11:27.)

According to Jesus, man needs finding. As he is, he is lost. (Luke 19: 10.)

According to Jesus, man needs freeing. As he is, he is bound. (John 8: 34-36.)

According to Jesus, man needs the principle of harmonious relationship with his fellow men. As he is, he does not admit himself to be his brother's keeper. (Matt. 5: 43 ff.)

And all these needs Jesus claimed that he himself would meet. His love was God's power unto salvation.

Jesus—Lord or Leader?

But precisely here arises the question about the nature of the relationship of Jesus to men. Did he claim to be Leader teaching men a way of life, or did he claim to be Lord over men's lives? Indeed, it is not so much a question of what Christ claimed for himself, as a question of his method with men. The problem normally comes to focus in a discussion of the Sermon on the Mount. "Here," it is said, "is the heart of the Christian religion. Here are the teachings that men must follow if they desire to be Christian." Let us look at the Sermon on the Mount and see what it says. (Matt. 5-7.)

JESUS: Blessed are the poor in spirit for theirs. . .

I: But what about me? I want to be poor in spirit too, and who will make me?

JESUS: Blessed are the meek. . .

I: But how am I to become meek?

JESUS: Blessed are the pure in heart. . .

I: But who will cleanse me?

JESUS: Ye are the salt of the earth. . .

I: But I have already lost my savor. I want to be salted.

JESUS: Ye are the light of the world...

I: But I must be lit.

JESUS: Thou hypocrite, first cast out the beam out of thine own eye...

I: But I cannot see. I am blind. I want someone else to pull out my beam for me.

JESUS: Yes, you do. In fact, you by yourself cannot fulfill these teachings. But I will fulfill them for you and in you. Ask and it shall be given you. Seek and you shall find. Knock and it shall be opened unto you.

The Sermon on the Mount is more a statement of what will happen to a man when he allows Jesus to get hold of him, than a statement of what a man must do if he is to follow Jesus.

In that crowd whom Jesus was addressing were some who were anxious to become his disciples. He was a new Rabbi and it would be fun following him! And to them he says, "Are you willing to be meek, to be long-suffering, to be persecuted, to turn the other cheek, to walk the second mile...? For that is what I will make you do if you follow me. I will change you and you must make up your mind whether you want to be changed."

There were others in that crowd who, as they listened to his words describing the NEW MAN, wished with all their hearts that they could be like that; and to them he says, "You can become like that. I will do it for you. Trust me."

But besides these two groups, there were also in that crowd men and women who wished to be like that; but who at the same time were unwilling to let Jesus do it for them. "He is only a carpenter's son. They say that he is not even an orthodox Jew.... And besides, if we commit ourselves to him, he will want to change us completely, while it is only a part of his ideal that we accept.... In any case, we will follow him, though on our own; and after all, following him is the main thing...." Is it? And are we able to follow him on our own?

The Sermon on the Mount raises also another question which is pertinent to this whole inquiry. And that is the question of practical results. The issue may be stated as follows:

JESUS: Except your righteousness exceed the righteousness of the Scribes and Pharisees, you shall in no case enter the Kingdom of Heaven.

I: But if it does, can I be sure of my place in the Kingdom?

JESUS: No. For your question itself is a sign of pharisaic righteousness.

JESUS: Whosoever shall smite you on the right cheek, turn to him the other also.

I: Will that make him desist?

JESUS: Not necessarily. But your concern is not so much to make him desist, as to be willing not to take offense.

JESUS: Lend not hoping to receive again.

I: Does that mean that God will help me to get back my own?

JESUS: No. You may not get it back at all.

JESUS: Love your enemies and do good to them that hate you.

I: Will that change them?

JESUS: Even if it does not, you must continue to love.

I: What then is the point of it all? I thought you were teaching a surer and better way, and a spiritual way of safe living, of achieving results.

JESUS: No. I am not concerned with what you call "results." Nor should they be your concern. Seek the Kingdom of God, not your place in the Kingdom, and His righteousness and all these things will be added unto you.

The Sermon on the Mount is not a new technique for achieving results, a new method of getting "there." It is just because it has been so adopted and interpreted by Gandhiji, as teaching a new technique and a new method, that the acceptance of Jesus as Lord still remains a problem in India. "Never mind plans and programs," Jesus seems to say; "let us first get related to each other. It is you I am concerned with. I want to bind you to me with a new relationship—the relationship of a man who builds his life upon me. I do not guarantee results. Indeed, you will not escape the storms or floods of life. But I do say this—your house will not fall. Your relationship with me will not be destroyed. Nothing will separate me from you or you from me."

What, then, about the floods and storms, and about making a world where they do not happen? Is the world never to be rid of its ills? Yes and no. For while every person who enlists as Christ's disciple is one more person to do battle against the floods, yet the world will never be safe and can never be made safe for those who will build their houses upon sand.

Thus the Sermon on the Mount is seen to be not a code of conduct given to men to follow, but a statement of issues which receive their ultimate validity, meaning and relevance only as they are recognized to be issues raised by Christ.

It seems that the early Church never taught the Sermon on the Mount to non-Christians. There is no preaching of the Sermon on the Mount in the Acts of the Apostles, for instance, nor in St. Mark's Gospel which sets out the preaching of St. Peter. The Sermon on the Mount was taught only after one had accepted Jesus as Lord. Indeed, the probability is that the Sermon on the Mount itself is a collection of the sayings of Jesus made by the Jerusalem Church for the instruction in the Christian way of those who were baptized. First the proclamation (Kerygma), then the teaching (Didache).

The paradox of the religious search—that was the starting point of this inquiry into the method of Jesus. How does he deal with life? What does he demand of men? But when these questions are answered, there is still one final question, "Show us the Father, and we shall be satisfied." To which he replies, "Have I been with you so long, and yet you do not know me?" "What do you think of the Christ?" "Who do you say that I am?" (John 14:8-9, Matt. 22:42, 16:15).

Man's discovery of God depends on his discovery of Jesus, and in his answer to the question which Jesus asks is involved his finding the answer to his own questions about God. Jesus is both God's question and God's answer to man.

3. *The Evangelist*

EVANGELISM is relating the Gospel to the torments of the world. But in so doing, no evangelist can seek to be greater than his Lord. "It is enough for the servant to be as his master." The methods which Jesus rejected as incongruent with his mission, the evangelist must reject too; the issue of personal discipleship to which Jesus pressed his challenge, the evangelist must press also. If the Gospel were only a truth, one could speak to convince; but, since it is the offer of life, one has to seek to persuade. People must be won into a willingness to receive. They must be awakened to their real need.

How is this possible? The possibility lies with God, but no Christian can serve this possibility except he himself be captive to the power of the Gospel. Only a heavy cloud can mediate the lightning. Only a person with an inner sense of compulsion can have compelling power. What is the nature of the Christian's compulsion?

I. SEPARATED UNTO THE GOSPEL

Paul, a servant of Jesus Christ, called to be an apostle, set apart for the gospel of God which he promised beforehand through his prophets in the holy scriptures, the gospel concerning his Son, who was descended from David according to the flesh and designated Son of God in power according to the Spirit of holiness by his resurrection from the dead, Jesus Christ our Lord, through whom we have received grace and apostleship to bring about obedience to the faith for the sake of his name among all the Gentiles, including yourselves who are called to belong to Jesus Christ; to all God's beloved in Rome, who are called to be saints: Grace to you and peace from God our Father and the Lord Jesus Christ. ROM. 1:1-7

We have entered a new era in which Jesus is King. A change has taken place within the very structure of history. There has been a decisive encounter between the prince of this age and the Prince of the age to come. A new realm of life has been opened up, the realm of light, which darkness cannot overcome and into which we are bidden to enter. But if all this is true, then it must mean a profound disturbance in the tenor of human life. It must cause a revolution in the life of those who are caught up by this Gospel. St. Paul, in the opening words of his letter to the Romans, describes this revolution. He there makes clear what the situation of the Christian is.

This letter is by St. Paul—a Jew and a Pharisee—and it is addressed to them that are in Rome—mostly Gentiles in the Imperial City. Why should St. Paul write to them? Because they are beloved of God, called to be Christ's men and women. The word "call" which St. Paul uses means "to call by name," it speaks of God's love for all and for each. It is important to emphasize this. The obligation under which we stand to love our fellow men is not what provides the evangelistic imperative. The evangelist addresses his audience as those whom God loves. The Gospel is theirs by right. We are but stewards of the mysteries of God. (I Cor. 4:1.) In the Diocese of Dornakal in India, it is part of the service of the baptism for every convert to place his hand upon his head and say solemnly, "Woe is me if I do not preach the Gospel" (I Cor. 9:16). The Gospel is gospel because it is meant for all mankind, and unless I partake in its outreach I do not partake in it at all. It is the love of God for others that lays its compulsion on the Christian and makes him an evangelist. He comes under this compulsion by tasting of that love himself. God who had called the nations has also called St. Paul: and in responding to God's call to him, St. Paul found himself involved in that wider call of God to others. That is how God's call to a person, which call is an expression of God's love toward him, becomes, when it is responded to, a call to apostleship.

An apostle is a personal emissary of God. He comes bringing God's message of love to men. All mankind are, as it were, walking toward God searching for Him; an apostle is one who has been converted, turned around, and sent forth. He comes from God toward men.

What message does he bring? The message that God has acted, acted on man's behalf; man's search is over and God has come to meet him. The evangelist himself is the promise of this meeting. That God has found him and sent him is itself a declaration of the love of God for those to whom he is sent. So does St. Paul speak of being "separated unto the Gospel": of having the boundaries of his life marked off by this activity of God. Evangelism is not something we do, it is something that God does. It is the going out of God's love. The Gospel is always present tense. And the evangelist is not merely one who proclaims, he is rather the means by which the Gospel becomes dynamic. He is God's Shaliach. When he acts God is acting. The Gospel separates him and gives to his life its distinguishing characteristics.

One of the first things which Constantine had to do after he became Emperor was to send priests to a tribe of Goths on the north shore of the Black Sea. The chief of the tribe had sent a deputation to him explaining that a Christian slave girl whom they had captured in a raid had converted them. A slave girl—there could be no better symbol of human helplessness: but because she was a Christian she belonged to that area of life whose boundaries are set by the operation of the Gospel. There the same power that raised Jesus from the dead was at work, and by her witness that power leaped out in dynamic activity.

We shake our heads at what are called mass conversions. They, at least, we feel are not examples of the working of God's power. But how does it happen that the people of a village, largely illiterate and therefore more closely bound to the past, are willing to take the god of their village shrine and throw him into the river, as the sign of their corporate decision to accept Jesus as their Lord? There is no triumph of the Gospel anywhere but bears the authentic mark of the power of the Resurrection at work. It is always God's doing.

But what about Constantine and the state patronage he offered to the Church? Or, if we would have an example out of our own time, what about the connection between the British Empire and foreign missions? One must confess to a feeling of dismay at the quickness with which some are willing to apologize for the way in which God has utilized human history.

Why cannot we see the power of God manipulating the events of the world, even as the Old Testament historian discerned it? If God used Constantine, that is no justification of Constantine: or if God used the British Empire is it in any sense derogatory to God? The task of evangelism demands that we keep in step with God who is as well the Lord of history as the Lord of His Church.

To be separated unto the Gospel is to have the activity of one's life determined by the operation of the Gospel, by the working of God wherever and however He may be at work. So that the first requisite of the evangelist becomes the experience of being caught himself in this working of God. We thus come back to St. Paul's theme, and his third word of emphasis: called—apostle—slave. Evangelism is not optional service for a Christian. We are not servants but slaves. We belong now to the Divine economy. Our life is not our own.

How do I come to this experience of enslavement? St. Paul came to it on the Damascus road when Jesus confronted him, and spoke to him saying, "Saul, Saul, why do you persecute me? . . . I am Jesus, whom you are persecuting" (Acts 9: 4-5). This experience of St. Paul is uncommon, but the burden of that experience is the burden of every experience of decision for Christ. It involves the recognition that Jesus died for me and that my sins put him to death. The call of God that found me came from the lips of One whom I had persecuted and denied.

Were you there when they crucified my Lord? I was there. I can see myself in each of the actors in that drama.

I was there in Caiaphas who would save the nation by letting Jesus perish. I was there in Nicodemus who would not risk his position in the Sanhedrin for Jesus' sake. I was there in Peter who loved but was unprepared. I was there in Judas who followed, but sought to bend Jesus to his own ends. I was there in Herod who did not care. I was there in Pilate who was afraid. I was there among the fickle crowd. I was one of the soldiers who simply did his duty.

I know I am guilty of his death. "This Jesus whom you crucified"—(Acts 2:36)—those were the words with which St. Peter faced his audience on the first day when the Church declared the Gospel: and those words were true. And it was only when I recognized them as true of me that I saw the meaning of the love of Jesus. He loved me and refused to depart from me even though I slew him. Now my life is his to spread abroad the message of his love.

> O let Thy love my heart constrain!
>   Thy love for every sinner free,
> That every fallen soul of man
>   May taste the grace that found out me;
> That all mankind with me may prove
> Thy sovereign everlasting love.[1]

In some such way the evangelist is constituted, through some such experience he comes to the knowledge that he is a slave of Christ. He is no servant selling his service for wages; he is a slave living on his master's bounty and serving his master's economy. (Sin gives wages, God gives gifts [Rom. 6:23].) He has but one commission—to commend the freedom of his slavery to those who know it not, to evidence the joy that comes by living within the bondage of this Gospel, to spread the area of influence of his Lord.

[1] Charles Wesley, "Would Jesus Have the Sinner Die?"

It is for this reason that St. Paul links grace and apostleship together. For apostleship becomes impossible where it is not supported by grace. The missionary has no merit of his own, it was God's love that found him: he is able therefore to commend that love to others. He is able to perform his task as an apostle and witness to God's grace, for he lives by it. He had stood by the roadside unemployed. Nobody wanted him. The Master who met him and set him to work in His vineyard did so out of the goodness of His heart. Grace has hired him and it is this very same grace that supports him as he works.

Grace made us apostles, grace keeps us in our apostleship. Otherwise we should run away in despair of accomplishing anything. For consider the task that is set us—the task of calling men among all the nations to the obedience that springs from faith. Faith is man's response to God's love. It is to learn to depend on God's faithfulness, on God's dependability. And because love has awakened faith, faith issues in obedience. "If a man loves me, he will keep my word" (John 14:23). Our task as evangelists is to mediate God's love so as to awaken faith. It is not our task, in the first instance, to invite men to obedience, to teach them Christian behavior. The Christian life is the life we live because we have become Christians. Obedience is gratitude for grace.

The good news, then, is this, that Jesus has been declared to be the Son of God. Humanly speaking he had a historical descent. But history did not produce him. He sojourned here. He arrived, the One whose arrival prophecy had foretold, and who at the last stood distinguished by the fact that he arose from the dead. This resurrection now marks the frontier where the Christian stands. Here, where life and death meet and life wins its victory, the Christian is caught and held by the calling of grace. Here is exercised that authority with which Christ was invested when he was manifest as the Son of God, and here the Christian finds that power operative which is the power of the age to come.

His call brings us to this frontier, his grace keeps us here, and here his peace stands guard.

II. WE WISH TO SEE JESUS

Some Greeks . . . came to Philip . . . and said to him, "Sir, we wish to see Jesus." . . . And they told Jesus. And Jesus answered them, ". . . unless a grain of wheat falls into the earth and dies, it remains alone; but if it dies, it bears much fruit. . . . Now is the judgment of this world, now shall the ruler of this world be cast out; and I, when I am lifted up from the earth, will draw all men to myself." JOHN 12:20-32

"This man receives sinners and eats with them"—the scribes and Pharisees said, murmuring against Jesus, to which he replied by telling them three parables. (Luke 15:2.) These parables are a classic description of what evangelism is. A man had a flock of a hundred sheep of which one was lost. The lost sheep must be found and restored to the flock. A woman had a head-chain of ten coins of which one was lost. The lost coin must be found and restored to the chain. A father had two sons but his home was broken. Both sons had to be won and restored to the home.

The recovery of wholeness—that is the purpose of evangelism, the bringing back of the lost to their place in the economy of God. For God so loved the world that He gave His Son, that no one and nothing may perish and become useless, but that everyone and everything may find their true usefulness in the purposes of God. (John 3:16.) The gospel must be preached to the whole creation, for that is what the Gospel is. It is God's address to creation as a whole, His action to bring to creation its harmony. (Mark 16:15, Col. 1:23.) Every activity, therefore, which seeks to effect this harmony is an activity within the meaning of the term "evangelism." It is part of the working of God. The school, the hospital, the rural center, the laboratory: these are all ways in which God is seeking to bring wholeness into life. No less significant are the ways he adopts through those to whom He has committed power. Through them He effects orderly government that those conditions may prevail in which the Gospel may spread (I Tim. 2:1-4), and through them also He effects those events which execute His judgment over sin (Luke 19:41-44).

It is a truth which we tend to forget that the God of whom the Bible speaks is a God who is at work in the world. "God made the world in six days and rested on the Sabbath day, you too therefore must rest on the Sabbath," the Pharisees said to Jesus. But Jesus replied that the work of creation was not over; "My Father is working still, and I am working" (John 5:17). When God rests Jesus shall rest also. The Sabbath is not a memorial of the fact that God has rested, it is an anticipation of the hope of God's rest— of that Sabbath when the work of creation shall be complete and the full harmony of creation shall have been accomplished. (Heb. 4:9.)

This working of God is the theme of the Bible, and it is set out on three levels.

There is the level of all creation taken as a whole. In the beginning God made the heaven and the earth, in the ending He will bring to pass a new heaven and a new earth. (Gen. 1:1, Rev. 21:1.)

Then, there is the level of the life of the peoples, of community. In the beginning God called Abraham that in him all the peoples of the earth might be blessed, in the ending there will be brought the glory and the honor of the peoples unto Zion. (Gen. 12:3, Rev. 21:26.)

And lastly, there is the level of the life of the individual. In the beginning God walked with Adam in the garden, in the ending God will be in the midst of His children—the host of the redeemed. (Gen. 3:8, Rev. 21:3.)

This total movement, which God initiates and empowers, is the movement of evangelism, the movement of God's saving activity in the world. And it is in this movement that *we* are called to participate when we are separated unto the Gospel. Our particular part is set within a total drama, our particular portion must be understood in terms of the whole. What is this part or portion? The answer can be summarized again in terms of the three levels that we have referred to.

On the level of creation as a whole, Christian evangelism involves every activity in which Christians are engaged. Where the Christian is in his normal day-to-day work, there is the frontier of the Gospel as it confronts the world.

On the level of community, Christian evangelism involves making visible in the world, and making effective, that community which oversteps every barrier and in which the wholeness of the future is already realized in part. This is the Church.

On the level of the individual, Christian evangelism involves effecting that introduction between God and man which will bring him into relation with the saving activity of God. Let us consider these a little more in detail.

The Christian Frontier:

If life as a whole belongs to God, then the Christian Gospel has relevance not only to the inner life of the Christian but also to his outer work. A Christian is called upon not only to be a Christian who is a lawyer, or a doctor, or a politician, or a man of business ... but to be a Christian as a lawyer, or as a doctor, or as a politician, or as a man of business. ... The Christian faith must impinge on the world and its affairs, and it is where the Christian laymen are that this process must take place. Evangelism awaits today a larger fulfillment of the functions of the lay Christian. The Church is a priestly body, it mediates the power and presence of God to the world, the task of mediation being one in which every member shares.

The Ecumenical Institute of the World Council of Churches, with headquarters near Geneva, has been founded to emphasize this aspect of the evangelistic task and to help in its fulfillment. It brings together periodically men and women engaged in the same profession in order that they may seek together a common understanding of the relevance of the Christian faith to their work. How is the Christian conception of Justice relevant to the work of a Christian lawyer, or the Christian conception of Personality relevant to the work of a Christian doctor, or the Christian conception of History relevant to the work of a Christian politician, or the Christian conception of Community relevant to the work of a Christian businessman. . . ? When the Christian laymen are able to make their day-to-day work Christian work, then will happen the greatest revolution of our time. The leaven must be hid within the meal if the whole is to be leavened. (Luke 13:21.)

This also is the specific evangelistic relevance of Christian community institutions such as schools, hospitals, rural centers and so on. These are not just means of service, they are not just means of establishing evangelistic contact between the Church and the community at large, they are essentially part of the impact of the Gospel upon the world. In the countries of the older churches where the general culture is rooted in the Christian tradition, the task of the Church normally would be to maintain and strengthen this connection so that the State itself could run most of the necessary community institutions: most, but not all—for the Church can never acquiesce in a State monopoly in this field. In the lands of the younger churches, however, the problem is the opposite. Here, only the Church is able to run community institutions which will represent the impact of the Gospel upon the world. Of course in time, the culture in a non-Christian country too can be permeated with a Christian outlook, so that the Church can concentrate part of its energies on providing Christian personnel to work in State institutions.

The point, however, of this discussion is not to deal with the relation between Church and State in this matter, but rather to emphasize why a Christian community institution is an evangelistic agency. It is an evangelistic agency in its own right as something which the Church must do, because it is the Church for the world. A Christian school, for instance, is more than a school which renders educational service. It is more than a means of getting into touch with people to whom we want to present the claims of Christ. It is more than a way of providing education for Christian children. A school is one mode of the life of the world, and that mode the Church must bring into captivity to the obedience of Christ (II Cor. 10:5). This is the function of the Christian school.

An African chief is said to have defined the problem of Christian education as similar to that of ivory hunting. "You go hunting ivory," he said, "and you find that there is always an elephant attached." That precisely is the problem of the Christian frontier. You start out to educate people in Christian faith and discover that you must educate them for all of life. It is the problem of dealing with the elephant in the process of getting the ivory.

The Christian Community:

The life of the Christian community as a community is and should be an evangelistic fact. It should be both a demonstration to the world of what the Evangel accomplishes and an instrument for the propagation of the Evangel itself. The Bible speaks of the Church as an instrument of the Kingdom and also as a foretaste of it. St. Paul describing the central act of the Church's life, and the act by which it lives, gathers together three truths in one sentence. "For as often as you eat this bread and drink the cup, you proclaim the Lord's death until he comes" (I Cor. 11:26). The Church lives by participation in the life of Christ. The sacramental act of this participation is a witness to the world of the death of Christ. This witness points beyond his death to his coming again.

This connection between the life and worship and witness of the Church is an essential connection, and part of the reason for the weakness of the Church's evangelism is that this connection is not explicit to the world. Participation in the life of Christ does not seem to issue in witness to the death of Christ on men's behalf. The Christian seems unwilling or unable to say, "Now I rejoice in my sufferings for your sake, and in my flesh I complete what remains of Christ's afflictions for the sake of his body, that is, the church" (Col. 1:24).

Also witness to the death of Christ, when it is borne, often seems unaccompanied by that joy in hope of his coming again. The central act of the Church is orientated to a past event—the last supper in the upper room; it is orientated also to a future event —the marriage supper of the Lamb. (Rev. 19:9.) There is need to make explicit to the world this community which, by the nature of its very existence, witnesses to an event in the past as the central event of history, and witnesses also to the certainty of an event in the future in and by which history will come to its culmination. The Christian community anchors human history to these two events, and anchorage is, above all, what the world needs.

Another aspect of the evangelistic validity of the Christian community is that its life is meant to be the new wine of God's extending Kingdom. It has been a necessary consequence that wherever this new wine has been put into old bottles, the bottles have burst. One hundred and fifty years ago Christian missions began to move in force into Asia; now one hundred and fifty years afterwards the old bottles in Asia have burst and Asia stands on the threshold of making new forms for her life. Today Christian missions are moving in force into Africa; tomorrow the shackles that bind Africa now will burst asunder. New wine will burst old bottles. It is meant to. (Acts 11:1-18; cf. Matt. 9:17.)

The Christian community represents, wherever it is in the world, the sovereignty of another King. It is always a parish, a group of those who are *paroikoi*—aliens (I Pet. 2:11), whose one controlling purpose is to increase the area of influence of their King. "We are a colony of heaven," St. Paul said, emphasizing the fact that the Christian community must live unconformed to this world, and commending by their life, to those around them, the life of their fatherland. (Phil. 3:20, Rom. 12:2.)

The Christian Individual:

At the heart of the Church's life there are the two sacraments of our Lord. The sacrament of Holy Communion is always celebrated in the plural—"the Body of *our* Lord Jesus Christ which was broken for you." In it the individual Christian comes to his Lord, not alone, but as a member of the whole family. The sacrament of Holy Baptism, however, is always in the singular—"I baptize *thee* in the Name of the Father, the Son and of the Holy Spirit." Here the individual stands alone, called by name and incorporated into Christ and his body.

This importance of the singular, nevertheless, tends to be forgotten in actual practice, especially as the Christian Church in any place gets older. Children are born into Christian homes, they are baptized, they are brought up in the nurture of the Lord. . . . So far, so good, but! I have two sons. I trust that they are growing up in a Christian home. But, I know that someday they must make their individual response to Jesus. How that day of encounter will come I do not know. I only pray that their mother and I may so teach them about Jesus and guide them in their relationship to him, that when Jesus comes to them with the demand for conscious discipleship they may each recognize him and say gladly, "Yes." This encounter may take place with or without a great emotional upheaval, it may not even be one event but a ripening relationship across the years: but whatever its form its inward quality before Jesus is the same—it is the experience of standing alone stripped of every disguise, of being shattered by his presence and stabilized by his forgiving love. It is the experience of the I before the Thou. The more moral my children are the more difficult they will find the consciousness of sin, but Jesus must deal with that. It is he who converts.

"Work out your own salvation," St. Paul says: that is what evangelism is. It is the receiving of salvation in that encounter with Jesus that we have been speaking about, and then the working out of this salvation "with fear and trembling; for God is at work in you, both to will and to work for his good pleasure" (Phil. 2:12-13). Evangelism is the working out of a working in.

There are those who conceive of the Christian life as a life of gradual withdrawal from the world. "Mysticism" is their key word. They want to lose themselves in the consciousness of the Divine presence. Here is no working out, it is only a working in. Basically this ideal is unchristian. The Christian ideal is "sonship"—the doing of the will of the Father. Sadhu Sundar Singh, when he was in England, wrote to his friends in India saying, "Pray for me because I am desperately tempted. I would rather spend all my time in prayer than go out and fulfill my engagements." Peter did not know what he was talking about when he said to Jesus, on the mount of transfiguration, let us build three tabernacles here. (Luke 9:33.)

And then there are also those who would plunge into activity sponsoring programs and plans for the making of a better world. The desperate need of our time is for those who are strong because they are humble, and who are humble because in their inward life they have been broken before God. What the world is faced with are the consequences of leadership which is ruthless because it is not strong. A modern pagan philosopher has said that what we need today is to recover a sense of cosmic piety. He was actually asking for something much simpler. What we need today is a sense of spiritual humility. The Church must produce the men and the women who have stood before God.

We began this discussion with a definition of evangelism as sharing in the activity of God, we have arrived at the conclusion of our discussion with a definition of evangelism as meeting the world's need by those who have met Jesus. To commend Jesus, to lift him up that men may be drawn to Him—that is the center of the evangelistic task. "Sir, we wish to see Jesus," they ask us, as the Greeks asked Philip, and it is to that question that ultimately we must provide an answer. The world needs every form of Christian activity, but no Christian activity can take the place of Christ himself. It is said that Lord Tennyson, visiting a village in Lincolnshire, was to be put up in the home of two simple Methodists. He arrived, and greeting his hostess remarked, "Well, what is the news today?" To which she replied, "Why, sir, there is only one piece of news that I know, the news that Christ died for all men." The poet answered, "Yes, that is old news, and good news, and new news, too." That is the news which must be shared with all men.

"Our fathers were impressed," says the report of the World

Missionary Conference at Jerusalem, "with the horror that men should die without Christ. We are also impressed with the horror that men should live without Him." Are we? A South Indian pastor was visiting some poor Christians of his parish. He found that owing to heavy rain the previous day, most of the huts were in ruins and the place itself just one big stretch of slush. What could he tell people in such a condition? It seemed a mockery to speak of a God who cares. And then there appeared at the door-way of one of the huts an old woman, and he said to her, "Amma! you all seem to be in much trouble here." And she replied, "Yes, Ayya! and but for Yesu Swamy [the Lord Jesus] we should not be able to bear it."

It is not cant—this talk of Christ as the need of the world. It is desperately true. Him alone circumstances cannot change, nor the world take away: and for him the world waits. "Yesu Swamy," it murmurs with a wistful yearning. Can we do anything to meet that yearning need?

4. The Church

EVANGELISM is the saving activity of God. That is a total definition. Evangelism is the impact of the Gospel on the world. That is a definition in terms of the circumference of activity. Evangelism is to meet the need of the world for Jesus. That is central. But where is Jesus to be found? He is to be found where he is at work, and he is distinguishably at work in the Church. The Church is his body.

We have tried to understand the compulsion on the evangelist by considering the nature of the call which constitutes him. We have tried, also, to understand the significance of his task by looking at the movement as a whole to which his task belongs. We must seek now to go further and penetrate into the reality of the life and function of the Church of which the evangelist is a member, and because of the nature of which he is an evangelist. The Church is not only an instrument of the Gospel but part of the Gospel itself.

I. THE PLEDGE OF OUR HERITAGE

Blessed be the God and Father of our Lord Jesus Christ, who has blessed us in Christ . . . before the foundation of the world. . . . In him we have redemption through his blood, the forgiveness of our trespasses, according to the riches of his grace. . . . In him you also, who have heard the word of truth, the gospel of your salvation, and have believed in him, were sealed with the promised Holy Spirit. EPH. 1:3-13

In these words St. Paul gives us a definition of the Church which relates the nature of the Church to the Activity of the Triune God.

The Church is the result of the Call of God.

The Church is the society where the healing processes of Christ are at work.

The Church is the habitation of the Holy Spirit, the agent of God's power in the world.

The Call of God:

The Church comes into being in any place only because the Church is already there in the call of God. A Church is not formed by those who hear the call joining together to form a Church, rather the call itself gathers together those who respond to it. The Church is not an association of those who are called, the association itself is what the call effects.

In the Eden story, the first words which God addresses to sinful man are: "Adam, where art thou?" (Gen. 3:9). This is more than a question. There is a sob in it. It is God's cry of sorrow at man's sin. This cry is a constantly recurring note in the Bible.

The ox knoweth his owner, and the ass his master's crib; but Israel doth not know, my people doth not consider. Is. 1:3

> How shall I give thee up, Ephraim?
> How shall I cast thee off, Israel? . . .
> My heart is turned within me,
> My compassions are kindled together. Hos. 11:8

O Jerusalem, Jerusalem! . . . How often would I have gathered your children together as a hen gathers her brood under her wings, and you would not. LUKE 13:34

The task of the Christian is to make actual this call of God. He reiterates it. And even as he is proclaiming it, it is sounding in the souls of his listeners. He only helps to make them conscious of it, to make them understand its significance and its urgency. He, then, stands by praying for them and persuading them until they answer the call with the obedience of faith. Preaching has saving power since it is dependent on the operative quality of the call itself. It has pleased God through the foolishness of the preaching to save them that believe, seeing that unto them that are called Christ is the power of God. (I Cor. 1:21-24.)

In the story of Isaiah, there is no specific call of the prophet himself. He simply overhears the sorrow of God as God seeks for messengers to send to do His work. (Is. 6.)

> In rhythm with the heart of the world
> The prophet's heart pulsates;
> In tune with God, his soul expectant waits;
> And lo, as if overheard,
> There falls upon his ear the Divine word,
> "Whom shall I send? And who will go for Me?"
> The wistfulness of that soliloquy
> Pierced through to the prophet's soul.
>
> God has not called him, but his heart is stirred:
> The longing of that sigh has like a sword
> Gone in.
> The need of the world, in God's heart, a cross.
> The cross of God becomes his prophet's call,
> And he must answer. So must also we,
> "Here am I—oh Lord, my God! send me!"[1]

Some families among the goldsmiths of one of the villages in South India had become Christians as a result of an intensive evangelistic campaign. A missionary in another village, not very far away, spoke to a goldsmith there about what his people in the other village were doing. "Why have you not become Christians?" the missionary asked, to which the goldsmith replied, "No one asked us." "Everyone who calls upon the name of the Lord will be saved. But how are men to call upon Him in whom they have not believed? And how are they to believe in Him of whom they have never heard? And how are they to hear without a preacher? And how can men preach unless they are sent?" And how can they be sent except that they first have been found? (Rom. 10:13-15.)

---

[1] D. T. Niles, "The Vision."

The Healing Processes of Christ:

Christ is the head of the Church, his body, even as the husband is the head of the wife. And he is himself its Saviour for Christ loved the Church and gave himself up for her that he might consecrate her, that she "might be presented before him in splendor, without spot or wrinkle" (Eph. 5:21-27).

The Church comes into being because of the call of God, it is what it is because of the working of Christ. Christ and his Church are one body, even as a man and his wife are one flesh. They are bound together in one life, Christ loving the Church and the Church responding to that love, Christ giving himself to the Church and the Church giving herself in return in receiving him. Thus is the life of union between Christ and his Church cleansed and sanctified.

To be a member of the Church, therefore, is to be within this process of life. It is to find oneself in a relationship to Christ which is redemptive; to be bound to him, in spite of one's sins, with the unbreakable bond of marriage, unbreakable because he will not break it. His forgiveness is the determining reality of this life of union, so real that it evokes repentance and unbinds the power of sin. Indeed, it is because forgiveness is not just a transaction between God and the individual, but a quality of the life of union between the Church and her Lord, that Christ taught his disciples so insistently that he who does not forgive cannot partake in forgiveness.

Here we sense the truth of the statement that the Church is not merely an instrument of evangelism but part of the Evangel itself. It is part of what God has done for man. In fact, in many of the villages of India, the Church is the first item of the Evangel which those poor and simple people accept. They find in its life a release from the oppression of centuries, and once in it they gradually discern what the springs of the Church's life are. They partake in its worship, and are led by that worship to understand and believe in the Lordship of Christ. It is easier, where the chance exists, to present the claims of Christ through worship than through argument.

But what about mixed motives in the case of people who have accepted the Church first? Are they not moved by the hope of the various social and economic benefits that will accrue to them by joining the Christian community? We can only answer in the word of the South Indian pastor defending the mass movements in India, when he said, "Thank God their motives are mixed. We should not be surprised if the only motive in the case of these people was material gain. But it is not. There is also the desire for spiritual peace." The life of the Church is an organic whole. It includes the love of the brethren, and if the benefits of that love are what draw men into the sphere of the Gospel, why should we say to them, Nay? It is one of the signs of our misunderstanding of the Gospel and the place of the Church in it, that we are so willing to set ourselves up as judges of the motives of men when they seek to enter the Church. It may be that they seek Jesus because of the loaves, it is for the Church to present Jesus as him of whom the loaves are a sign. (John 6:26.)

The life of the Church comes by union with Christ, and men share in it as they deepen in their acceptance of God and of Jesus. "And this is eternal life, that they know thee the only true God, and Jesus Christ whom thou hast sent" (John 17:3). "To know" is to enter into a marriage union, the old single life is over, it is a new creation.

The Habitation of the Spirit:

This unity of life between Christ and his Church is the means by which the world is to be redeemed. It is a foretaste of the life of glory. It is the redemptive encounter of the Holy Spirit with the world. The worldly habitation of the Holy Spirit was a long time in preparation and was accomplished only with the resurrection of Jesus. When Jesus rose from the dead, death became a breached wall, and a present experience of the life of the world to come became a permanent possibility. The new creation came into being, that which was the result of the union between the risen Christ and his Church, and this new creation became the habitation of the Holy Spirit. For the Spirit was not given until Jesus was glorified (John 6:39), but when he was glorified then did the Spirit come to reside in the Church. (Acts 2:33.) Jesus himself had asked his disciples to wait in Jerusalem for the coming of the Spirit. (Acts 1:8.)

In the life of the eternal city God will be present with His people. There sin and death shall be no more, neither will there be sorrow nor parting. (Rev. 21:1-4.) But a foretaste of this life is available now, a pledge of our heritage and an installment of it. We experience it in the Church when the Church confronts the world in the power of the Holy Spirit. The existence of the Holy Spirit in the Church is not a static existence, an existence that can be taken for granted; rather, it is a dynamic existence, an existence in the Church when the Church is the Church. Power is only for witness.

The Holy Spirit gives power.

In the New Testament, power is the capital letter of the Church. Early Christians preached with power convicting the world of sin. They announced with power breaking the bonds of sickness. They challenged with power casting out the spirits of evil. Where is this power now? Where is the evidence of the promise of Jesus, "He who believes in me will also do the works that I do; and greater works than these will he do, because I go to the Father" (John 14:12). The power is still surely there, but unused: for only minimum power is necessary as long as the Church is content to restrict the scope of its witness.

The call of God is unto all the nations. Let the Church in any land limit this call by imperfect obedience and the power of God in any full measure becomes unnecessary for its life. The healing processes of Christ by which the Divine forgiveness issues in health and wholeness are for men in every aspect of their life. Let the Church in any land be remiss in extending and mediating this healing influence, and it throttles the power of God in its own life. The experience of the Holy Spirit comes in the encounter of the Church with the world. Where that encounter is partial, either in extensity or intensity, the experience of the Holy Spirit is partial also.

Only as we obey the command of Jesus to be his witnesses do we learn the significance of his promise, "Lo, I am with you always, to the close of the age" (Matt. 28:20).

II. HE CHOSE FROM THEM TWELVE

The scribes and the Pharisees . . . were filled with fury and discussed with one another what they might do to Jesus. In these days he went out into the hills to pray; and all night he continued in prayer to God. And when it was day, he called his disciples, and chose from them twelve . . . . to be with him, and to be sent out to preach and have authority to cast out demons. LUKE 6:11-13, MARK 3:14

The Church exists by mission. It is bound by God's Word which created it, when God said to Abraham, "I will bless thee . . . and be thou a blessing: . . . in thee shall all the families of the earth be blessed" (Gen. 12:2-3). But the children of Abraham miscon-strued their calling. They looked upon their blessing as a privilege and refused to recognize their mission. God called and recalled them to their specific responsibilities as His people, but they would not hear: until at last disaster overtook them, and they found themselves in exile in a foreign land. "Why must God use a nation more wicked than we to punish us?" they asked; while those among Israel who had remained faithful to God asked the question, "Why must we also suffer with the rest of our people who have been faithless?" To both questions the prophet of the Exile gave the same answer. "Accept your suffering as a fulfillment of your vocation," he said, "and the day will yet come when the nations will say, 'Surely he hath borne our griefs, and carried our sorrows; . . . the chastisement of our peace was upon him; and with his stripes we are healed'" (Is. 53:4-5).

But it was not to be. When Israel returned from exile, the old cancer was still shown to be alive. The book of Jonah, written in protest against this tendency, is the last book of the Old Testament recalling Israel to its true mission. Then, in the verses from St. Luke's Gospel with which this chapter begins, we see them standing at the parting of the ways. The leaders of Israel had rejected Jesus and sought to destroy him: Jesus answered by rejecting Israel. No one could have missed the significance of his action when, from among his disciples, he chose twelve men. Here were the patriarchs of the new people of God, here was the nucleus of His new ecclesia.

He called them apostles (Luke 6:13), those who were sent forth. They were men bound by a mission. On them had devolved the promise and the command to Abraham. No man lights a lamp and puts it under a bushel, but on a stand and it gives light to all the house. (Matt. 5:14-15). If a man is not so foolish, God is not less wise. Neither will He light a lamp and put it under a bushel. However, if a lamp will not accept the lampstand, then not only is the lampstand removed but the light also goes out. "I will . . . remove your lampstand from its place, unless you repent" (Rev. 2:5)—that is the awful truth about the nature of the Church.

One of the great historic creeds of the Church, formulated in A.D. 325 by the Council of Nicaea, assigns four attributes to the Church. It is One, it is Holy, it is Catholic, it is Apostolic—all of them attributes that spring from a universalism which is integral to the Church's nature.

The Church is One:

This is because its Lord is one, and its life is a life of union with its Lord. "Has Christ been parcelled out?" asks St. Paul of the Corinthian Christians who enjoyed the luxury of sects. (I Cor. 1:13 Moffatt.) The Church's mission springs from this Oneness. It is the Church's task to lead all God's children into this unity of life. But (and that is why the movement for Church Union is so closely linked to the missionary movement) this unity of life which is both the basis and the end of missionary work is already broken. It is not a question of Church Union for the sake of administrative and program efficiency, it is rather a matter of restoring full circulation of the sacramental life of the Church through all its parts. Those who seek Church Union on practical grounds often forget that Church Union can never be a human achievement. They need to remember that the task is to make visible a unity that already exists rather than to create a unity which does not exist. But neither do those who seek Church Union on the basis of theological truth arrive anywhere unless they are dominated by the missionary concern of the Church. Israel rejected Christ because it would not expose the riches of its heritage to the strain and stress of missionary endeavor. It sought to guard its possessions and crucified the heir. (John 1:11.)

We have said that the goal of Church Union movements is more than the achievement of administrative unity. It is necessary to emphasize also that it is other than the achievement of such unity on a world scale. The unity of the Church comprehends regional differentiation. The Church among any particular people is the Church for that people. It belongs there while it is also part of the One Church of Christ. It must affirm its belonging to the Universal Church, it must also express its involvement in the vocation of the nation for which it is the Church. As the Proposed Scheme for Church Union in Ceylon puts it: "A regional scheme of union should preserve in that region the principle of the unity of the Body of Christ. Also, the liberty of a regional Church has enabled, and may in any place enable, the God-given genius of great nations to find appropriate expression in the worship and work of the Church; and so the riches of the nations are carried into the City of God, there to be hallowed by His acceptance and recreated by His Spirit."

Here is the theological basis of the problems of adaptation which a missionary has to face. Here is the argument for insisting that missionary-sending agencies cannot direct missions except as they try to understand the life and destiny of the peoples among whom they work. God's activity is always in history as a whole as well as in the Church. Indeed, we see again and again a synchronization of events which teach us how God works. That Church Union in South India should come in the same year that India regained her political freedom, that there should be a major missionary occupation of Africa at the same time as Africa has become strategic in international relations—these are no less significant than the synchronization which we see when we consider that Israel was ripe for judgment at the same time as Babylon and Egypt, her neighbors on either side, were at the height of their rivalry, or that the Gospel of Jesus was launched on the world when the peace of Rome had provided it with roads and ships and with orderly government, and when the culture of Greece had provided it with a common language.

There is a tendency for missionary agencies to be concerned exclusively with the Church in the missionary land rather than with the land itself, and to think of their work in terms of sending money and replacing personnel. There is urgency for an understanding of the hour at which a people stand as a people in the working of God, before the Church among that people can be made relevant to that hour.

The Church is Holy:

Jesus chose his disciples "that they might be with him"—that is the basis of the Church's unity. He also chose them "that he might send them forth"—that is the basis of the Church's holiness. A thing was holy when it was holy unto the Lord, separate for His use, peculiarly His own. The Church is holy because it is the instrument of God's mission to the world. He separates it from the world in order that He might address it to the world. Let a Church cease to be missionary and it ceases to be holy, it ceases to fulfill the function for which it was wrought. Spiritual holiness comes as a result of the Church being true to its primary function. A missionary Church is constantly renewed in its life because God is working through it and in it. Self-preservation is the theme of a constantly recurring crisis in the life of the Church. "Unless a grain of wheat falls into the earth and dies, it remains alone; but if it dies, it bears much fruit" (John 12:24). It is more than symbolic that Christ's first prediction of his passion followed closely on his foundation word about the Church, and that Peter's first temptation soon after was to deny the necessity of the cross. (Matt. 16:18-23.)

What, then, is the relation of the Church to the world, the relation unto which the Church is separated, and in maintaining which the Church is renewed? It is a threefold relation, a relation of stewardship, intercession and mediation.

The Church is the Steward of God's bounty for man and it is part of the Church's function to see that this bounty is fairly distributed. In some countries the Christian community itself possesses the power to control such distribution, in other countries the Christian community is a small minority but nevertheless possesses means of influencing a just distribution. This function of the Church to control or influence the just distribution of God's bounty is largely exercised outside the councils of the Church itself in the legislative halls of the nations, but it is a function of the Church nevertheless. A Christian college, for instance, is a discharge by the Church of its stewardship. It distributes thereby God's bounty of knowledge. But, thereby it sends out too into the life of the general community, persons influenced by Christian ideas and ideals, persons who, in the public life and the administration of the State, will themselves influence a juster sharing of God's good gifts among all His children.

The relation of the Church to the world is also one of Intercession. It must constantly pray not only that larger justice shall prevail in the affairs of men, but that men may learn, when they get their share of God's bounty, that it is God's bounty in which they share. When the State provides for free medical treatment, it is seeking to do justice by all its citizens: but when a man receives health he is receiving a free gift of grace. It is the task of the Church to pray both that God's blessing may rest on every endeavor to promote the well-being of man as man, and also that men may be moved so to accept God's gifts as to be grateful to the Giver. (Matt. 5:16.) That *is* gratitude. It is the act of receiving the giver as well as his gift; and God never gives gifts without seeking to give himself along with them. Jesus cured ten lepers but he was satisfied that his work was done only in the case of the one man who came back and gave God thanks. (Luke 17:17-18.) Those who minister in Christ's name must maintain this distinction in their own minds. They must serve where service is needed, but they must judge their success not by how much service has been rendered but by how many have been led to God. It is essential that the Church support its program of service with earnest intercession that those who profit thereby may be led to Christ.

Lastly, the relation of the Church to the world is one of Mediation. God is not only the God of creation who has provided in His world sufficient bounty for man's well-being, He is also the God of redemption who has provided in the Church a foretaste of eternal life, which is the life of the age to come. A revealing example of the way in which the three functions of the Church interlock—and the function of mediation is shown as a distinctive function of the Church—can be given as follows: Medical healing is a general provision of God in creation. The Church exercises its obligation of stewardship by running hospitals. It is also God's will that His gifts should be a means by which His children are led into right relations with Him, the Giver. The Church exercises its obligation of intercession unto this end by appointing hospital chaplains. But, in addition to this, God has provided in the life of the Church the means of "wholeness"—wholeness of the whole man, body and mind and soul. "Is any among you sick? Let him call for the elders of the church, and let them pray over him, anointing him with oil in the name of the Lord; and the prayer of faith will save the sick man, and the Lord will raise him up; and if he has committed sins, he will be forgiven" (James 5:14-15). The sick man is saved not just cured. He is made whole.

The Church is Catholic:

Creation has lost its wholeness. It groans and travails, awaiting its redemption. (Rom. 8:22.) The Church is addressed to the world as God's redemptive act for the recovery of wholeness. (Eph. 1:10.) Let the Gospel be preached to the whole creation. (Mark 16:15.)

Here is the Church's charter to concern itself with the totality of God's world. God's will must prevail in the whole of His creation, and the Church's task is to work for this fulfillment. This world is meant to be a home for man, and the prophet does rightly when he makes the wilderness blossom as the rose (Is. 35:1-2) and the animals of the forest lie down together in peace (Is. 11:6-7) as part of his picture of the world when man attains his deliverance. The correlation of the life of nature with the redemptive activity of God is amply manifested in the story of the deliverance of Israel from Egypt, as well as in the story of the ministry of Jesus when he was in the flesh. But the Church cannot be the means of wholeness for creation if it is not in itself whole. To be Catholic is to be whole. By its very nature there is demanded of it that it actualize this wholeness in its life, work, marks and mission.

The Church must recover wholeness in its life. The consequence of a divided Church has been its inadequacy. To give two examples: it is not just coincidence that there is a revival of the healing ministry of the Church at the same time as there is the swelling of the Ecumenical Movement, nor that evangelistic results follow where a congregation is renewed by a larger wholeness in worship and witness. Evangelism is an overflow of the Church's life, not a mere program of activities.

The Church must recover wholeness also in its work. An example of the implication of this can be given by quoting the description of a Christian hospital in Africa which an African doctor gave in one of the sessions of the Amsterdam Assembly of the World Council of Churches. This is the substance of what he said: There are no other hospitals within a radius of about a hundred miles. So when someone falls ill in one of the outlying villages, he is carried to the hospital by his relatives. At least eight men are needed to carry the sick man in relay. It may take about four or five days to reach the hospital, and some women accompany the men to cook for them along the way. When they arrive at the hospital all those who have accompanied the sick man live in the homes near the hospital. The sick man gets well in about five or six days. And they all go back to their village. What has happened? First of all, about ten people have been away from the village for about fifteen days. This means that there are so many hands short in the fields for so many days, and those who have been away lose at least a month's food as a result. Secondly, the African homes near the hospital are always full up with visitors and their home life is completely disrupted. And thirdly, the sick man when he gets his next attack of illness feels that the demon whom he cheated last time by going to the white man's hospital must at least be appeased now. "A Christian hospital is not Christian simply by being a hospital," this African doctor said; "it is Christian only when it is part of a total approach to the problems of African life."

The wholeness of the Church depends also on whether it bears all the marks of the Church. The Church is like a beam of light. A Church in any place is a cross section of that beam. The cross section must catch all the colors of the spectrum. The part must be according to the whole (*Kata Holos*—Catholic). Some Churches are yellow, orange, red; some just violet, indigo, blue; some only purple. They are all cross sections, all Churches, but not all whole. The movement for Church union is an attempt to recover this wholeness. And lastly a Church is Catholic only as it is for the whole, for all men. Neither race, nor class, nor color, nor nation can be a qualifying factor of the Church, even of a Church.

Unfortunately, in a theological sense and according to theological history, the word Protestant has come to be used as the opposite of Catholic. But the true opposite to Catholic is Sectarian.

The Church is Apostolic:

The disciples were chosen to be with Him—the Church is one; they were chosen as the new Israel—the Church is holy; they were chosen for the preaching of the Gospel to all the world—the Church is catholic; they were also to carry authority—the Church is apostolic.

There are differences of opinion as to how this authority is maintained, what the content of this authority is, and the means by which this authority is transmitted: but there is no controversy with regard to the basic fact that the Church is apostolic, God's personal messenger to the world. The Church is not a messenger by substitution as if it acts on behalf of God. It is rather a messenger by embodiment, God is always acting, and the Church embodies this acting of God in a special way.

It is this element of apostolicity which constitutes also the givenness of the Church, and invests it both with its freedom and its bondage. The Church is not free to change the content of the Gospel, the content of the Apostolic witness. Often, particularly for the evangelist, the temptation will be strong to make modifications in the Gospel which will make it both more acceptable and more reasonable, modifications that will take out of the Gospel its offense. But this temptation must be resisted. The Jews found the Gospel unacceptable, a stumbling block; the Greeks found the Gospel unreasonable, foolishness—but St. Paul was resolved to proclaim it as it was. (I Cor. 1:23.) The task of the evangelist, as far as he is able, is only to make the Gospel understandable.

But a missionary especially from one land to another must also take account of the freedom of the Church. He must beware lest he confuse the Christian culture of his country with the Gospel. The Gospel is seed which, when it is sown in the soil of a country's life, brings forth a plant. The plant is Christianity. It bears the marks both of the seed and of the soil. There is only one Gospel, but there are many Christianities, many cultural forms in which men express their Christian faith. It is inevitable that the missionary should bring a pot plant, the Christianity of his own culture; it is essential that he allow the pot to be broken and the plant to be rooted in the soil of the country to which he goes. "For what we preach is not ourselves, but Jesus Christ as Lord, with ourselves as your servants for Jesus' sake" (II Cor. 4:5)—that is the missionary ideal. Perhaps another word, with respect to the calling of the missionary, may not be out of place here; a word just to emphasize the desirability of the missionary calling being looked upon as a calling to serve a people and not only as a calling to do a particular work. It should not be possible for a missionary to speak too easily of leaving one country and going to another.

In all things the apostolicity of the Church is the canon of the evangelist.

We began this chapter with the words, the Church lives by mission; we have seen now how determinative of the missionary function of the Church its essential qualities are. Thus by the Church's life and expansion is witness borne to the increasing purposes of God, and the Church itself made manifest as His body "the fullness of him who fills all in all" (Eph. 1:23).

5. The Task

EVANGELISM is a way of the Church's life. Evangelistic work is the way the evangelist lives. As our next step we shall collate many of the things we have already discussed and state them in relation to one another as describing this evangelistic way. It is a way of sanctification, it is for our sake. But sanctification is in order that they may believe, it is for their sake. Their believing makes manifest the glory of God, it is for God's sake. "I pray," said Jesus, "for those whom Thou hast given me, for they are Thine; all mine are Thine, and Thine are mine, and I am glorified in them."

God's glory is the end of evangelism, an end that will be accomplished when that glory is revealed in fullness when Christ returns. Time looks forward to this end and derives meaning from it. As we understand this, we shall see the urgency of the evangelistic task as well as perceive its true dimension.

I. A SLAVE TO ALL

Woe to me if I do not preach the gospel! For if I do this of my own will, I have a reward; but if not of my own will, I am entrusted with a commission. . . . I have made myself a slave to all, that I might win the more. . . . I have become all things to all men, that I might by all means save some. I do it all for the sake of the gospel, that I may share in its blessings. I COR. 9:16-27

The object of evangelism is conversion, conversion to Christ and personal discipleship to him. But involved also in this conversion are conversion to the Christian community and conversion to Christian ideas and ideals. All three conversions must take place, even though the order in which they take place may be different. Thus in India with its mass movements the first conversion is largely to the Christian community—proselytism. Then takes place conversion to discipleship—evangelism. And then along with it and because of it follows conversion to Christian ideas and ideals—Christianization. In Christian colleges the order of conversion is usually different. First of all, it is Christianization, then evangelism, and then proselytization. In the case of those driven by spiritual hunger or despair due to the consciousness of sin, the first effect of the Gospel is evangelism, their being won to personal discipleship to Christ, and then follows proselytization and Christianization together.

It is futile and perverse to isolate these three movements of the soul from one another and treat them in opposition to one another. They belong together, each makes the others possible, and they derive meaning from one another. "But surely you can go to heaven without joining the Church," someone says; or, "You are a Christian when you lead a good life whatever your theology of Jesus," someone else asserts—and the discussion comes down with a bang to the level of what we ourselves think should be. We have extricated ourselves from the world of Biblical thought and have begun to talk what we call common sense. But the Bible persists with its challenge. "What kind of a world is this?" it asks, "and, if it is a world in which God is at work, then, is not the demand on us that we be obedient and not merely good? Goodness can be irrelevant, rightness or righteousness is what is wanted." So that we are back again in the world of the Bible seeking to grapple with the basic Biblical truth that God is a working God, and that Jesus is God's deed of deeds.

Both in the New and Old Testaments, sin is described in a specifically religious way. A sinner is one who is out of step with God. He is in the wrong place. But we so often use the word "sin" purely in its moral sense, to denote just defects in character, that we miss the real significance of the Biblical horror of sin. To sin is to refuse to meet God at the place where God has come to meet us. It is an act of ingratitude, of disobedience and of self-assertion. God has come to meet man in Jesus Christ, and, because God has done this, the question becomes urgent—"What have you done about what God has done?"

Again and again in India and Ceylon those who do evangelistic work are asked the question, Have you a Gospel for Mahatma Gandhi? Is he not morally a greater man than you?—Yes. Has he not deeper spiritual insight than you?—Yes. Have you then a message for him?—Yes, the same message. What have you done about what God has done? It is a question that all men must answer; and in the face of that question, moral excellence and spiritual insight are not truly pertinent.

The argument makes God's activity its starting point, and, because it is God's deed, Jesus cannot be an option for man. The necessity to bring men to Jesus Christ, therefore, as the place and person where God has willed to meet them, and in discipleship to whom they will walk in obedience before God, having fellowship with Him in the work He is doing, is what dominates the whole evangelistic process.

We can now seek to summarize the qualities which must characterize such a process.

Proclamation:

This will naturally be the first characteristic, for the standing ground of evangelism is an activity of God which is to be proclaimed.

It is proclaimed because it is God's deed. A leading Brahmo Samajist in India once delivered an address on the subject "Jesus, my Ishta Devada"—"Jesus the God of my choice." "I worship Jesus," he said, "I worship Jesus only, but I am a Hindu. I am a Hindu because I accord the right to every man to worship the God he chooses." That is true Hinduism. Christian faith, on the other hand, is not built on my choice of Jesus, it is built on my response to Jesus' choice of me. The initiative is his, and he claims me by the right that he made me. I was his all the time.

The necessity of proclamation arises also from the fact of stewardship. Very often, when we speak of evangelism, we talk about sharing with other men what we have found in Jesus. There is partial validity in this position, but only partial; indeed, so partial as to be almost invalid. The compulsion on the evangelist arises not so much from his experience of the Gospel as from the nature of the Gospel itself. Every time I look at the Gospel I know it belongs to my fellow man and that I have to pass it on. Jesus died, and my fellow man is my brother for whom Jesus died. When Paul says, "Woe to me if I do not preach the Gospel," he does not mean, "If I do not preach the Gospel, some day God will punish me;" he means, "If I do not preach the Gospel, I shall myself perish without experiencing the power of the Gospel now." In order to be experienced, the Gospel must be passed on. "If I say, I will not make mention of the Lord," said Jeremiah, ". . . there is in my heart as it were a burning fire shut up in my bones" (Jer. 20:9). We have not realized what the Gospel is if we have not felt the compulsion of stewardship with respect to it. "I am entrusted with a commission, a stewardship," said St. Paul.

There is still something more implied in speaking about proclaiming the Gospel. It is that the Gospel is Gospel not when it is believed but when it is confessed. The rock on which the Church is built is not Peter's confession but a confessing Peter. Where the Gospel is believed and confessed there is a Church. The Gospel is something operative, dynamic, something that is doing something. Lock it up and it ceases to be Gospel, good news.

Identification:

This is a necessary characteristic of the evangelistic way since it carries into effect the logic of the incarnation.

"I have become all things to all men," says St. Paul. He found no other way to carry out his commission, to fulfill his stewardship. There is no other way. We cannot commend the Gospel to our contemporaries unless we can enter into their frustration and their expectation; and then address the Gospel to ourselves as we stand in their situation. If we will listen to Hindus until Hinduism becomes a temptation to us, if we will listen to Communists until we feel the attraction of Communism, if we will listen to Muslims until Islam begins to attract us, then we shall be in a position to get the Gospel across to them. Are we not surprised to read that Jesus was tempted in all points like as we are? (Heb. 4:15.) He so identified himself with us that he felt the force of our temptations. He shared our situation. He sat where we sat. (Ezek. 3:15.) This is what identification means.

It is said that Professor W. E. Hocking once asked C. F. Andrews the question, "How do you preach the Gospel to a Hindu?" To which Andrews replied, "I don't. I preach the Gospel to a man." You have to get within the Hindu until Hinduism becomes your context, and when you have got there, in that situation you do not meet the Hindu but the man. You are then able to preach the Gospel to the man and not to the Hindu in him. If anybody exemplified this method of preaching the Gospel, it was C. F. Andrews himself. Actually it is wrong to call this a method of evangelism, it is so intrinsic to the evangelistic way.

This indentification, however, is not achieved easily, nor is it achieved often unless it includes indentification as far as possible with the cultural ways of those to whom one seeks to present the Gospel. This is something which the missionary from one land to another especially needs to remember; and particularly women missionaries, for women seem to be culturally more conservative and find adjustment to another culture more trying.

Demonstration:

This characteristic of the evangelistic way is an explicit result of the dynamism of the Gospel.

One of the unforgettable moments for me at the Amsterdam Assembly of the World Council of Churches was when in his address Bishop Stephen Neill looked at that imposing gathering and said, "When did you last try to lead someone to Jesus?" In my own heart that question created fear. It had been so easy to get swept into positions of administrative responsibility, with work in committees and councils, and to fill one's time with preaching the Gospel from platform and pulpit, that the day when one sat side by side with a person, wrestling with him and for him that he might find Jesus, had become an experience of the past. But as long as that remains an experience of the past, and Christian work has become exclusively an impersonal dealing with the mass, then the Gospel ceases in large measure to be known in its operative reality. To demonstrate the Gospel is, to use the words of St. Paul, to partake in its demonstration, and every other form of demonstration must be supported by this elemental form where person with person meet and, in that meeting, the Gospel is experienced as God's power unto salvation.

There is another emphasis included in this word "demonstration," and that is the emphasis on the life of the evangelist himself. That which counts is not the witness of the things one does or refuses to do, but rather the witness of the fragrance of one's life. It is possible to bring oneself to behave in a certain way when dealing with other people, but the fragrance of one's life is the fragrance that is truly there. With respect to it, dissimulation is impossible. Also, just as there is the fragrance of the life of an individual, there is the fragrance of the life of a Church. Someone has said, "There was a time when a disobedient Church could commend the Gospel. That time is now past."

"We Christians have the unmistakable 'scent' of Christ, discernable alike to those who are being saved and to those who are heading for death. To the latter it seems like the very smell of doom, to the former it has the fresh fragrance of life itself" (II Cor. 2:15).[1]

Interpretation:

This is important because evangelism is useless where the Gospel is not made understandable and meaningful.

[1] From *A Translation of the New Testament Epistles* by J. B. Phillips.

The Gospel is a mystery even though it is an open mystery. In it we have:

> Royalty hidden in a stable.
>
> Universality hidden in an exclusive race.
>
> True Divinity hidden in a man who experienced every human need and temptation.
>
> True Humanity hidden in a life of miracle—of spotless purity, stupendous authority and marvelous works.
>
> Voluntary self-giving hidden in a murder.
>
> Truth hidden in parables.
>
> The Resurrection hidden by its transcendence over common human experience.
>
> And eternal contemporaneousness hidden by a life lived in the process of time.

But why? Why this hiddenness? Christ himself gives the answer when he says in the words of Isaiah: " 'You shall indeed hear but never understand, and you shall indeed see but never perceive' " (Matt. 13:14). He who would be "Lord of all, or not at all" has made it impossible for men to apprehend him with only a part of their personality, lest "they perceive with their eyes, and hear with their ears, and should turn again." It is the task of the evangelist who has come to understand the Gospel because he has brought to it the discernment of faith to interpret that Gospel to others.

But interpretation depends also on the use of significant language. When I was in the United States of America some years ago, I was invited to a theological school to address the students. Instead of addressing them I said to them, "You are learning to preach the Gospel, I want you to preach the Gospel to me. Think of me as an American pagan. I have never been to church. I have never read the Bible. The home from which I come is also pagan. I have an elementary education. I am a worker on the road." The first thing those students said to me was, "You are a sinner." To which I replied, "I don't know what you are talking about. I have never heard the word 'sinner' before. . . ." It is unnecessary to describe here that whole meeting, but for fifteen minutes those students preached the Gospel to me, while I kept on saying, "I don't understand. Please use words that I know." They finally ended by saying, "Such pagans don't exist."

They do, and unless we learn to use language that our hearers understand and words which have the right emotional overtones for them, we remain but poor interpreters.

Transformation:

This is the objective of evangelism, the conversion experience which it seeks to achieve.

The presentation of the Gospel must be transforming in its results, transforming on the hearer as well as on the speaker. We may never forget that the call to apostleship is linked to the call to sainthood: and that we shall become saints only through the discipline involved in being true apostles. As for the hearer, he cannot be transformed except as the Gospel makes connection with his mind and his soul. We have already spoken about this, but two more words may here be added—first of all, to insist that the presentation of the Gospel be made relevant to the hearer, and, secondly, to express the warning that simply telling the truth of the Gospel may not be meaningful proclamation at all.

There is held in Ceylon every year in August a Buddhist festival called the Perahera, at which the relic of the Buddha's tooth is taken in procession. There is a mammoth crowd, and among the crowd hawkers go around selling sweets and fruits and drinks. At one Perahera, there was noticed also a hawker selling, "Cherry Blossom shoe cream." The shoe cream was all right, but it was completely irrelevant to the occasion. Nobody bought it.

A man went about telling everyone whom he met, "The world is round like an orange." He kept on announcing the fact until the police removed him to a mental hospital. He told the truth, the truth he spoke had meaning, but it was not a meaningful proclamation of the truth at all.

Transformation depends on establishing connection.

Proclamation, identification, demonstration, interpretation, transformation—"Who could think himself adequate for a responsibility like this?" "Only the man," says St. Paul, "who refuses to join that large class which traffics in the Word of God—the man who speaks in the Name of God, under the eyes of God, as Christ's chosen minister" (II Cor. 2:17).[2] "Lo," says Jesus, "I send you out as sheep in the midst of wolves" (Matt. 10:16). But he is the Shepherd not only of the sheep but also of the wolves.

II. THE MORNING STAR

"I Jesus have sent my angel to you with this testimony for the churches. I am the root and the offspring of David, the bright morning star." The Spirit and the Bride say, "Come." And let him who hears say, "Come." And let him who is thirsty come, let him who desires take the water of life without price. . . . He who testifies to these things says, "Surely I am coming soon." Amen. Come, Lord Jesus! REV. 22:16-20

The Morning Star has appeared and it will soon be dawn. This fact and this hope set the perspective for our work and for our thought, as they determine the nature of time itself.

Time is God's time. Before Jesus came, it was the period of preparation for his coming; now that Jesus has come, it is the period of waiting until he comes again. Time is in length what God decides it shall be, and it is filled with the activity of God. All around the world, every time someone writes down the day and month and year he is saying something about Jesus Christ. He is saying that so many years have passed since Jesus Christ was born. Jesus is the center of time. He is also the end of time, for time will cease when he comes again in glory. Time will then have been fulfilled.

What is the significance of this for us as we seek to understand the nature of the Christian task?

[2] *Ibid.*

First of all, that time comes to us laden with destiny. Time is not a vacuum that we can feel as we like with whatever we should like to do. Time belongs to God and every moment of it carries with it His will for us. What we do is our answer to this will: and by our answer our destiny is set. "Be strictly careful then about the life you lead; . . . make the very most of your time. . . . understand what is the Lord's will" (Eph. 5: 15-16, Moffatt).

Secondly, that time comes to us charged with direction. God is at work, and time flows from His act of creation to His act of incarnation, and from His act of incarnation to His act of consummation. So that when we handle time we are, as it were, bound to deal with it according to its grain. To attempt otherwise is merely to produce splinters. Jesus said, "He who is not with me is against me; and he who does not gather with me scatters" (Luke 11:23).

And, thirdly, that time comes to us challenging decision. "Today, if you should hear his voice, harden not your hearts" (Heb. 3:15). "Now is the acceptable time: now is the day of salvation" (II Cor. 6:2). This is the basis of the urgency which characterizes the Christian life. Time is always present tense in the presence of God.

The Biblical writers were so controlled by their recognition of this quality of time that the historical record which they give us is determined by it. Every event is first set by them in its chronological place and is explained on the plane of human free will. This is the plane of *chronos*, of time as sequence. Here events take place as a result of human activity or of natural phenomena. Empires rise and fall, battles are lost and won, individuals live and die, peoples appear and disappear, human causes are established or thwarted. . . .

But the whole history of human living stands under the eternal will of God. God is concerned with the world He has made. So that every event, while it takes place on the plane of human free

will, also takes place under the eye of God. It has a vertical reference. The function of the prophet was to bring this vertical
reference to bear on every event and to pronounce judgment on it
as an event that happens in a world which belongs to God and
where God is King. This plane of reference is the plane of *aiōnios*,
the plane of the eternal will of God.

To say that God is King, however, is to say not only that Kingship belongs to Him but that His Kingship is maintained. His
sovereignty is effective in the world. He determines the ends which
our human actions shall serve. We think to establish our own
purposes but God manipulates human events for the accomplishment of His will. The plane of *aiōnios* supervenes on the plane of
chronos until time is fulfilled, each event is fulfilled time—*kairos*
—carrying God's decision and holding within it the promise of
the future.

To give two examples:

> The Jewish exile in Babylon was an event in *chronos*. It
> was due to the rise of the Babylonian empire and the rivalries
> thus aroused. But it was conditioned by the judgment of God
> on the sin of the Jewish people. Here was the vertical reference
> of the event to *aiōnios*, the plane of God's eternal will. It
> marked the end of a period and the beginning of another in the
> history of God's redemptive action. It was *kairos*, decisive ful-
> filled time.
>
> The crucifixion of Jesus was brought about by the interplay
> of many human interests. It was an event in *chronos*. It was also
> in "the definite plan and foreknowledge of God," an event that
> had its origin in *aiōnios*. It occurred when the time was fulfilled
> and the hour was come—when it was *kairos*.

In a study of the theology of evangelism this Biblical conception of time is important because the strategy of evangelism must
finally be based on one's apprehension of *kairos*. The world is full
of crying needs, and our times are so full of clamant questions that
the temptation is strong to dissipate effort in doing everything.

It is essential to discern the strategic issue, to make clear the problems which hold the promise of the future. As Dr. John R. Mott has often emphasized, the necessity is for the Church to have a mobile strategy. The Church must throw its forces where the enemy is weakest and a break-through is possible, and where the enemy is strongest and strong defense is necessary. To scatter our resources holding on where we have begun simply because we have begun, is to forget that it is a war in which we are engaged. If we are hard pressed it means that we are pressing the enemy, if we are comfortable it means that we are behind the lines. It is always *kairos* somewhere.

The other truth is that it is not the same *kairos* everywhere. Those who were at the Amsterdam Assembly of the World Council of Churches had this borne in upon them very strongly. Indeed, there we discerned the interlocking significance for the Church of the double fact that in every country the Church was conditioned both by the historic moment in which that particular country stood, as well as by the historic moment which was peculiar to the Church itself. We recognized at Amsterdam that though there was one world, there were also many worlds. Historically, politically, economically, socially not all parts of the world were at the same hour. The tasks of the Church and of Christians in Africa were different from those in Britain; the choices facing the Church and Christians in America were different from those in Czechoslovakia; the mood of the Christian faith in India and China was different from that on the European continent. But we recognized also at Amsterdam that though the Church in every land was facing a different hour, there was an hour that characterized the Church as a whole. History determines the frontiers of the Church's tasks, but the Church as the Church creates also one of the world's frontiers. We are asked to show the relevance of the Christian faith to the world's needs and problems—a relevance that must be stated differently in every concrete situation; but we are also under God's command to call men to live relevantly, relevantly to God's ongoing work and His purposes. It is not enough to spread the theological butter on political bread. It is necessary that men who are asking the Church to prove to them that God is relevant should be bidden by the Church first to become themselves relevant to God. As the churches in our various countries we stand at different historic moments facing different tasks. But also, as the Church we stand together in the same historic moment, for the task of the Church everywhere and always is simply to be the Church.

Here are a series of pictures in which Amsterdam made me think of this world, and its problems, pictures which seem to me to define the nature of the moment in which different parts of the world are; and because of this definition, pictures which suggest also the tasks the churches face. As one looks at Europe it seems as if Europe is in its time of harvesting. The wheat and the tares have grown together, but now the harvesting has come. Nothing can be done by the nations to prevent the angels of God from setting their sickles to the harvest. But when the wheat has been gathered and the tares have been burned, the gathered wheat will become again the seed for a new sowing. God's hour has come for a fresh gathering together of the remnant in Europe. In East Asia, on the other hand, one seems to be standing at the moment of the triumphal entry. The older churches in the West are the ass and the younger churches in Asia are the colt of the ass on which the Lord comes. The abuses of the temple market will soon be attacked, but beyond this there await both Calvary and Easter. In Africa, new wine is being put into the old bottles of racial attitudes between colored and white, as well as of the tribal life of the African peoples themselves. Already one can see the old wineskins being eaten into, and the day will not be far when they will be burst. While in America, the picture that one sees is of a patchwork garment—new cloth sewn on old, perilously near to tearing.

To evangelize is to have undertaken to discern the times, to follow where God is at work, and to prepare for Christ's coming. We run with patience the race that is set before us, looking unto Jesus who is its author and waiting for him who is its goal. (Heb. 12:1.)

There is only one certainty about the future, and that is that the future belongs to him. "He will come" is the only future tense in the Church's creed.

At the close of his address to the Christian Youth Conference at Oslo, Bishop Berggrav pointed upward to the ceiling of the cathedral in which we were met, and said: "Did you observe the ceiling of this church? It is low and heavy. The atmosphere is made oppressive. Why is it like this? Surely, there is no such intention in it, but as a matter of fact, it becomes today a symbol of the whole situation of men. I wish I could take away this temporary ceiling, now eleven years since it was put in. Then you would see the most lovely and mighty scenery, prepared through these eleven years by one of our Norwegian painters. He needed this temporary low ceiling as the floor of his workroom. In one year we hope to have the view of what is above. Then you will have the most convincing sermon which painting can give of Christ the Lord. But you could not see it today, just as it is not given to us today to see Christ as the actual Lord of the world. But He is! When the low ceiling of life in time is taken away, you will get to know that He was there all the time, and that the low ceiling of today was His working floor."

He will come, the ceiling of this life will be lifted, and then we shall see what our great God has accomplished.

6. The Non-Christian

EVANGELISM is witness. It is one beggar telling another beggar where to get food. The Christian does not offer out of his bounty. He has no bounty. He is simply guest at his Master's table and, as evangelist, he calls others too. The evangelistic relation is to be "alongside of" not "over-against." The Christian stands alongside the non-Christian and points to the Gospel, the holy action of God. It is not his knowledge of God that he shares, it is to God Himself that he points. The Christian Gospel is the Word become flesh. This is more than and other than the Word become speech. The religious quest for self-realization is henceforth pulled up with this demand, that the self is not realized by a flight from the finite and the temporal, but by taking its stand at the point where the finite and the infinite, the temporal and the eternal meet.

I. BUT YOU NEVER KNOW

"Truly, truly I tell you, no one can see God's Realm unless he is born from above.... What is born of the flesh is flesh: what is born of the Spirit is spirit. Do not wonder at me telling you, 'You must all be born from above.' The wind blows where it wills; you can hear its sound, but you never know where it has come from or where it goes: it is the same with everyone who is born of the Spirit." JOHN 3:3-8, Moffatt

There is always an unpredictability about the way in which the Gospel becomes effective when it is proclaimed. This is more so where the Gospel is addressed to those of another faith. For where there is another faith the Gospel must necessarily relate itself to that faith both in judgment and in fulfillment. What we shall attempt in this chapter is to explain this relation; remembering, however, that thereby we do not make the effectiveness of the Gospel less unpredictable but only help the evangelist to make the mode of its address more adequate.

For the purpose of our discussion we shall choose Buddhism as the non-Christian faith we shall deal with; and also in order to give directness to our discussion, use the device of a letter written by a Christian to a Buddhist. Were I writing to a Buddhist seeking to make an introduction to the presentation of the Gospel, what should I say? How would I explain the perspective of the Christian when he views another faith? Here is how I should attempt it:

This letter is written to you, a Buddhist, by me, a Christian. That means that it is written by one who accepts the life and teaching of Jesus Christ as affording the key to the fullest and most adequate understanding of life and its meaning. But also since this is a letter written to you, who are a Buddhist, I have sought to establish a relation between what I want to say and what you already believe. Besides, this letter is only an introduction. It must be followed by a positive statement of the Christian faith. You can be assured that when I make that statement I shall try to put it into language and thought forms which are familiar to you. It will be inevitable, of course, that though words and ideas will be familiar, you will find them set in a context often different and sometimes even contradictory to their natural context in Buddhism.

The Truth of Buddhism:

Perhaps this letter had better begin with a question which I am sure you will want to ask. Have I the right to use words and ideas which belong to one religion in order to express the truths of another? Is not every religion a whole, and do not ideas in it derive their meaning from their place in the whole? The question is legitimate, but my answer must be that in using words and

ideas, so derived, there is no intention to graft into the Christian
faith elements of truth as I see them in Buddhism; but only the
attempt to state the Christian faith in language that already has
significance for the Buddhist. There is also a second answer on
which this first answer is dependent, the answer that when I, as a
Christian, came to study Buddhism I found that it fertilized my
faith and enriched my understanding, so that these Buddhist terms
and ideas have come to have a real meaning for me in the context
of my own faith. This is what my faith too leads me to expect, for
it asserts that God has not left Himself without witness among any
people, and that it is in the purpose of His design to gather up all
things in Christ in the fullness of time. (Act 14:17, Eph. 1:10.)

Religious truths do not meet in the library, they meet in the
minds and souls of men; so that, while to some extent a student
can approach the study of a religion neutrally, he can never completely or even adequately do so. Thus I cannot formulate any
general theory as to the relation between the Christian faith and
the Buddhist *Dhamma*; all that I can do is to present my faith as a
Christian to you as a Buddhist in as meaningful a language for you
as I am able to use, and then leave it at that.

But I can do one other thing also, and that is to share with you
frankly my own appraisal of Buddhism as a Christian student of it.
Among the great religions of the world, Buddhism is one of the
most realistic. It does not suffer from any cheap optimism either
about man or about the world. Man is conceived of as man, without any attempt to invest him with quasi-divinity; and the world is
accepted as it is without any attempt to rationalize or minimize its
tragedy. Besides, the whole paraphernalia of practices by which
men seek and have sought to invoke the intervention of the super-
natural is markedly absent. The result of this whole attitude is that,
positively, we have presented in Buddhism a diagnosis of life's
problem which is radical in its insight, and, negatively, we are set
free from all conceptions of God which treat Him as a *deus ex
machina*. It is right that a god whom men can manipulate should
be jettisoned.

The peculiar faith of Christianity is that there are two points of view from which every truth must be approached—a human point of view and a divine. There is the truth as man sees it from his predicament as man, and there is also the truth as God reveals it to man in terms of God's own purpose for man and for the world. So that the whole truth lies in holding together both these under one insight. Thus, life judged from the human end alone leads men either to a dreaming about utopias or to a renunciation of life's responsibilities; while life judged from the divine end alone leads men either to a dreaming about millenniums or to a denial of the reality of our temporal existence. The whole truth is affirmed only when it is recognized that we may not speak about life without speaking simultaneously both about man and about God, and about man as man and about God as God. Indeed, we state both sides of the truth only when we state them in tension—man in tension with God, and God in tension with men—for to fuse both together, as we do when we disguise man with divinity or enmesh God in human systems, is to destroy both.

What strikes me as a Christian student of Buddhism is that I find in Buddhism a description of life and the world from the human side without any attempt to camouflage the human situation; and also I do not find in Buddhism all those presuppositions about God as viewed from the human end which in other religions constitute such an obstacle to God's approach to man.

The Claims of Christ:

This is not to say that I believe that you as a Buddhist will find it easy either to understand or accept the truth of the Christian faith. You will not. For the whole point of Buddhism is the denial of the relevance, if not the existence, of this other side to life, the side which we have called divine. A study of Buddhism can fertilize the growth of understanding of the Christian faith, it can make for a formulation of Christian truth in Buddhist terms; but Buddhism as such affords no foundation on which the Christian faith can be based. In fact, when you face God as the Christian faith presents

Him, you do not face Him as a Buddhist but as a man; and you will find what all other men have found—whether they be Christians or Buddhists or Hindus or Muslims—that when the self comes to its decisive meeting with God the chief hindrances to accepting Him are the truths that it already knows and the goodness which it already possesses. One of the greatest Jews of his day found it to be so and expressed his experience in the words, "But whatever gain I had, I counted as loss for the sake of Christ. Indeed I count everything as loss because of the surpassing worth of knowing Christ Jesus my Lord" (Phil. 3: 7-8).

I have said all this to you, because it is only fair by you and myself and the nature of God's confrontation that I should give you this warning. I dare not minimize the contradiction that there is between the axiom of God and your natural presuppositions. God cannot be proved; to attempt to do so will be as futile as to attempt to prove color to a blind man. All that one can do is to show that the belief in God is reasonable, that it is on the basis of such a belief that life is seen to be most meaningful, and that there is ample witness for the truth of such a belief in the living experience of men and women of every age and country and kind. Let me help you to say, "I wish it were true": and then I know that you will see it to be true, because God Himself will give you sight.

Please do not misunderstand what I have said to imply that I think that you as a Buddhist are peculiarly blind, and that unless your blindness is cured you cannot appreciate truth in its wholeness. What I have tried to say rather is that you are blind exactly in the same way in which we are all blind, until we realize our blindness and ask that God give us our sight. Whether we call ourselves Christians or Buddhists we know and see this material life, and tend to deny any other reality, at least in practice. It is when we become convinced of our own helplessness and the world's hopelessness that we cry out for and receive both help and hope.

The Christian, when he receives his sight, begins to see the truth of many of the things which his religion has been teaching him all the time, and which he so far had tended to deny; the Buddhist, when he receives his sight, begins to see that the many things which he accepted as true are only partially so, and only true in a new context and in relation to other truths.

I wonder whether you think that I am presumptuous in saying this? Perhaps I am; but the determining faith with which the Christian approaches any truth is the faith that Jesus Christ is the fullness of light. (John 1:9.) This is not a claim that the Christian makes on behalf of Jesus; it is a claim which he himself made. He called himself "the Light of Life." So that in Christ's presence everything is seen clearly and in its right proportions and relations. In the presence of light, only darkness melts away, everything else remains. Hence arises the possibility of a statement of the truths of Buddhism within the context of the Christian faith, and also a statement of the Christian faith in Buddhist terms. In many cases the Christian context is revolutionary to the Buddhist concept, and yet the concept remains true; only before this, its truth was mis-stated because it was stated from the human angle alone.

In saying this, I do not forget that, for you, the chief difficulty will be to accept that there is any other angle except the human; and I should not be surprised if you thought sometimes that this belief in a divine order of reality is simply a way of escape from the hardness of this life, a way of achieving compensation. My only answer is that those who have truly found and accepted God in Christ have also found that thereby they have been committed to a life such as Jesus himself lived: and as you know, it is difficult to use the words "escape" and "compensation" about his life. Besides, if the truth be that there is a real escape from the tragedy of this life, real compensation and not phantasy, something that brings to this life true purposefulness and the courage to achieve, and also gives assurance to our hope for a more abundant life after death, then it were folly to discredit it.

The Nature of Truth:

As I said at the beginning, this is only an introduction, an attempt to explain to you the Christian perspective in general. There must follow a discussion of the various dogmas of our faiths.

A first question, however, can be dealt with straightaway, that which concerns the nature of dogma.

Every religion has its own dogmas—the unproved and unprovable assumptions on which its whole outlook depends. You may demur, and say that we must not assume anything without proof; but I would like to ask you what you do mean by proof after all. If by proof you mean that we must not believe in anything, whose existence cannot be demonstrated in terms of the knowledge we already possess, then I should like to ask on what grounds the knowledge we already possess is assumed to be adequate so as to afford a criterion of proof. On this definition of proof we should be able to believe neither in God nor in *Nibbana*. If, on the other hand, by proof you mean that we should not believe in anything which cannot be made the subject of a demonstrable experiment in life, then I should gladly consent; only I could not agree that this would be proof at all, for such an experiment merely amounts to judging of the nature of something by its effects without getting to know the cause of these effects directly and integrally. If, then, we are committed in every religion to the acceptance of dogmas, how do we decide between them? For decide we must, since the dogmas of the various religions are not mutually consistent.

Thought always must have a starting point in an axiom, and when we look at any religion we find that it takes its stand on a group of dogmas which are independent, and from that stand it seeks to explain life and its significance. When I say "explain," I mean that it seeks to relate the facts of life to its dogmas. That is what "explanation" ultimately is. A thing is explained when its relationship to something else which is more directly known is demonstrated. So that a religious explanation of life means that, beginning with certain dogmas, the relationship between the various experiences and facts of life are set forth, the explanation returning ultimately to the dogmas.

True thought is always circular, it must lead up to its assumptions: and the difference between one circle of explanation and another circle is a difference of radius. Some explanations are so narrow that they leave much unexplained, especially much that is important. The adequacy of truth in one religion as against another is judged according as the circle of explanation of that religion includes the largest number of significant facts.

In an article in the Buddhist Annual of Ceylon 1930, Buddhism is defined as "that religion which without starting with a God leads man to a stage where God's help is not necessary." That is true; it is also inevitable. If we do not start with God we shall not end with Him, and when we do start with Him we do not end with the doctrines of *Anicca, Anatta, Dukkha*. The existence of God means the existence of an order of life which is eternal—*Nicca*; that there is postulated for the soul—*Atta*—an identity which is guarded by God's sovereignty; and that sorrow—*Dukkha*—is seen to consist not so much in the transitoriness of things, as in the perverseness of our wills which seek these things instead of the things which are eternal. The circle of the Christian faith can thus be described as that which starting with God leads man to the realization that God alone affords the most adequate base for the most meaningful explanation of life's most significant facts.

You will probably notice, in this description of Christianity, that there is a use of the words "significant" and "meaningful" which is undefined. On what basis does one judge that this fact is more significant than that, or that this experience is more meaningful than another? Is there any basis at all for such judgment, or is not the truth rather this that such judgments are purely relative and personal?

Here we come against a further problem which must be clarified if we are to talk intelligently about truth at all. If, in our thinking about these large questions which involve the explanation of life's meaning, we necessarily think personally, then one man's answer is as true as another's, and there is no absolute standard of truth. A certain idea strikes one man as true because it "clicks" with the kind of man he is, and a contrary idea appeals to a man with a contrary character. We think with our character, and thought is not neutral. True thought, therefore, depends on true character.

In other words, there can be no such thing as absolute truth unless there were also such a thing as absolute goodness. And it cannot be a thing either, for goodness is personal.

We thus see the decisive significance for thought itself of the existence of God who is both truth and goodness and the standard for both; and we are able to say that thought is true which is the thought of a good man. This must not be misunderstood to mean that a good man can think correct mathematics. It means rather that where "truth" is concerned (truth not facts—truth is interpretative of life) goodness is its criterion. Once deny, however, that there is a God, and there is no escape from a utilitarian conception of goodness and a relativistic attitude to truth.

This drama between the relative and the absolute was once played out in its final terms when Jesus stood before the Roman procurator, Pilate. To Pilate there was no such thing as truth, it was a question of what served. To Jesus, however, the determining fact was the truth which he served and which demanded from him the supreme sacrifice. "I am come to bear witness to the truth," said Jesus; to which Pilate replied, "What is truth?" (John 18:38). What is truth indeed but God, and we think truly when we think God's thoughts after Him.

Through long ages religion has been man's attempt to question the universe and wrest an answer from it as to its meaning: God was asked to justify Himself before man, his needs, his problems, his desires, his standards; and in the result, men have either shaped God in their own likeness, that is, to suit their prejudices; or they have denied God's relevance and even His existence. When you study the Christian faith, however, you will find that basically the position is reversed. It is man who has to justify himself before God and His purposes and His standards. The meaning of man's life is not in himself, man is made for God; and men achieve their true destiny when they fulfill God's purpose for them.

Jesus is the revelation of God's purpose. In him God confronts man and challenges him. True enough, Jesus has to win our allegiance; but in the final result we shall find that it is we who have to win his approval. He is the standard both of goodness and of truth. Truth cannot be a teaching, it has to be a person; for truth and goodness must cohere. Jesus lived among men, and they beheld his glory full of grace and truth. (John 1:14.)

In Quest of Meaning:

I have said that the adequacy of a truth depends on how large the circle is of significant facts which it explains. I must now go further and say that it is not you nor I but God who should decide what facts are significant. In other words, those facts are significant for life about which God has spoken; and those facts about which He has not spoken are incidental. An example will make the meaning clear. There is not, for instance, in Christianity any explanation seeking to show that the experience of suffering is ordered by justice (this is what the theory of *Kamma* is meant to do); but on the other hand, the Christian does seek to invest the experience of suffering itself with meaning. Instead of treating suffering as an evil to be justified, it deals with suffering as a fact to be used. The determining motif is man's need of redemption and God's act to redeem him, and everything else, including the fact of suffering, is brought into relation to that motif. To anyone interested in the problem of suffering as such, this point of view of Christianity must necessarily seem disappointing; and yet for the person who has actually to deal with suffering, his own or another's, the Christian faith is full of meaning and of hope.

It is in an example such as this that one sees also most clearly the basic difference between Christianity and Buddhism, a difference that I must now try to state as plainly as possible. The difference, it seems to me, is this: the Buddha saw that life was meaningless in itself, and set out to rescue men from this meaninglessness. Jesus, on the other hand, saw that life could become meaningful in God and set out to call men to share that meaning. Your fundamental choice, therefore, is this: Whether you would live life only free from meaninglessness or also full of meaning. This is a fateful choice and an inevitable one.

Let me give you an example of the difference it will make to you as to which path you choose. Think of Ceylon and the future of our people. History is moving on and every race is struggling to live as meaningfully and as abundantly as possible. This is the criterion by which a people's progress is judged. But do you agree that it should be so judged? And why should you agree, if life's primary task is to escape life's meaninglessness? A Christian, on the other hand, does speak of God as the God of history, as One whose purposes are being wrought on the historical plane. Race and nation are religious categories to a Christian. They have validity within the purposes of God. He who brought Israel from Egypt brought also the Philistines from Caphtor and the Syrians from Kir. (Amos 9:7.)

Thus, as a Christian, I am forced to take the life of my country and of my people seriously; I am bidden to do so by my faith, which also sets for me the perspective according to which I must think and act. Nationalism for me is a Christian duty, it is also bound by Christian standards. You too probably are a nationalist, most of us do take the nation seriously these days, but then you cannot be a nationalist as a Buddhist. You can be a nationalist only as a Ceylonese. Race, nation, history—these are outside the Buddhist circle of explanation of life's problem; to the Christian, however, they are significant facts and find inclusion in his faith.

I know that this difference in terms of meaning which I have pointed out between Buddhism and Christianity can be denied. For few Buddhists do in actual practice live as those who merely seek freedom from meaninglessness; they live, rather, as meaningfully as they can. Besides, the doctrine of the eightfold path lends support to this positive attitude. Yet the fact remains that the Buddha does treat death as life's appropriate adjective—"All the constituents of being are transitory, work out your salvation with diligence"—(Mahaparinibbana Sutta) while for Jesus it is not death but life which characterizes life. "I came," he said, "that they may have life, and have it abundantly" (John 10:10).

Do I mean to say, then, that the life of the Buddha too was

lived in terms of meaninglessness? No, for the Buddha dedicated his life to rescuing men from the despair and disillusion into which contemporary Hindu religion had led them. His was a protest against the cheap optimism engendered by the belief in the cosmic soul, against the fruitless salvation promised by the practices of formal religion, against the irresponsible freedom sought along the way of ascetic renunciation. The Buddha had a mission in his contemporary scene, hence the charm and strength of his life.

But no protest, however profound, can be turned into a religion; a religion demands primarily something to profess and live by rather than something to protest about and live against. For when the self has done protesting, it inevitably comes to its rude awakening under the challenge of life for responsible living. We can side step that challenge for a time, but it has to be met, and be met on all levels. Adequate religion means that it shows us the deepest level on which to meet life's challenge—the level of reality, of life's inner structure, of life's true base.

It is in the exposition of this level that the fundamental differences of the various religions lie, and it is about this that they have their different dogmas.

II. FIRE UPON THE EARTH

I came to cast fire upon the earth; and would that it were already kindled! I have a baptism to be baptized with; and how I am constrained until it is accomplished! Do you think that I have come to give peace on earth? No, I tell you, but rather division. You know how to interpret the appearance of earth and sky; but why do you not know how to interpret the present time? LUKE 12:49-51, 56

I was presenting the claims of Christ to a Hindu audience in one of the towns of India when, at the close of my address, someone said, "The Christian religion is arrogant. Why cannot you state the teachings of Jesus in harmony with the teachings of other religions, without stressing what you call the uniqueness of the person of Christ?" "Your question," I replied, "is the common question of

India. Sri Radhakrishnan speaks of the claim to uniqueness in religion as an obsession of the Semitic mind. But I am in no position to surrender that which is not mine. I am not presenting claims which I am making on behalf of Christ, but only explaining the claims which he made for himself."

Who is Jesus? That is the central issue in any attempt to understand the relation between Christianity and other religions. In this chapter we shall restrict ourselves to a consideration of this issue in the form in which Hinduism poses it, for it is the Hindu for whom the equality of all religions is a dogma. Such a dogma is natural to Hinduism, since basic to Hindu thought is the conception of pantheistic immanence. To the Hindu, God is by definition both transcendent and immanent. And because He is immanent, immanent in all things, there is a basic unity of all existence and all experience. Differences exist in an undifferentiated essence. The transcendence of God is a consequence of this immanence. He is always other and always more than the modes in which He is known and experienced. If we should attempt to state the Christian position with regard to God's transcendence and immanence, we should state it practically in converse. The transcendent God wills to be immanent. His immanence is an act of grace; and wherever there is such immanence there has taken place a *Kenosis,* an emptying on God's part. Jesus is God who so emptied Himself that He became man. God's immanence is a result of His activity in His creation seeking to redeem it from sin. It is the liveliness of the Christian conception of sin which has saved Christianity from misunderstanding the truth of God's immanence and concluding in a belief in an undifferentiated essence. "Sinners? It is a sin to call a man so; it is a standing libel on human nature," so said Swami Vivekananda at the Chicago sessions of the Parliament of Religions. That is the true voice of Hinduism.

Having cleared the ground somewhat by this preliminary discussion, we may now address ourselves to the main issue of this chapter: Who is the Christ? and why must we proclaim him to the Hindu? Since this is not a new question but a very old one, a simple way of answering it would be to recollect the answers that are normally given to it and to consider them.

A first answer that is commonly given can be stated somewhat as follows: *"I have found something valuable in Christ and I cannot but share it with my brother."* But what does "cannot help" mean? Is it simply that the joy of our discovery flows over and demands to be shared? We know we mean more than that. It is the compulsion of a conviction that others are seeking for the very things we have found, and that we must tell them how they may find them too. But suppose there are other ways of finding what we have found— what then? It is an issue we should not dismiss as merely hypothetical, and especially when we know so well what it costs a man to change his faith. We know the price a convert has to pay, the sacrifice of things grown dear through years of association, the breaking of home relations which are the most sacred to any man. In the face of this, have we the right to call upon men to do this thing?

It will not do to say that Christ himself predicted that this would happen. He did say that because of him father would be set against son and mother against daughter (Luke 12: 52-53), but can we take that as the charter of our right to set father against son or mother against daughter, provided we satisfy ourselves that we are doing it in the name of Christ? We have no right to cause all this upheaval in the lives of men and women, simply because we have found something valuable in Christ and desire to share it with our brethren. We have that right only if it is true that Christ alone can give what we have found in him.

So we pass to a second answer that is often given to the problem we have set ourselves, the answer that *we proclaim the way of Christ because Christ alone can satisfy the spiritual longings of the human heart.* But what are these spiritual longings that Christ has satisfied for us which we claim that he alone can satisfy? Forgiveness of sins, a sense of security in life, the experience of daily guidance, a dynamic for moral victory, a power for present service—all will agree that these are among the commonest and the most insisted upon by Christians as what Christ has done for them. But is it true that we alone who follow Christ can and do speak of our spiritual experience in these terms? What about Manickavasagar, for instance, as burdened with a sense of sin he pleads for grace to wipe that sin away, and in his extremity turns to Siva who drank poison that the world might not be destroyed? Or what about the sense of security in life based on an experience of God as "all in all" which breaks through in the songs of Tiruna-vakarasu? And what about Mahatma Gandhi himself, who in our own day testified to an experience of daily guidance? Or still again, what about the modern emphasis on service and sacrifice as the characteristic experience of a devotee of God, which is found in the writings of Tagore? "Come out," he says, "of thy meditations and leave aside thy flowers and incense! What harm is there if thy clothes become tattered and stained? Meet him and stand by him in toil and in the sweat of thy brow."

What is our answer to these testimonies so like ours, so like the testimonies of countless Christians? "But you have picked and chosen your examples," some might say. I have, but they were there to be picked. "Much of this is due to the percolating influence of Christianity itself," many of us might affirm—but what is the force of that contention? Many Hindus themselves agree that Hinduism, as it is today, has been profoundly influenced by Christianity. What they are concerned about, and we also, is the question of conversion. "Christ alone can satisfy the spiritual longings of the human heart" is the answer we are considering, and in the light of what we see and know and hear, can we say Yes to that proposition?

There is a third answer given to the question we have raised, and given by a group that feels the difficulties of the two answers we have already considered. This is what they say: "*We dare not argue about it, for has not Christ himself told us to make disciples of all the nations, baptizing them in the name of the Father and of the Son and of the Holy Ghost? And besides we ourselves have heard his call in our own hearts.*"

But would there not be a strong probability that we have mis-understood our Master's meaning if we were unable to substantiate our right to ask men to follow him with a declaration of his uniqueness? As for feeling a call within our own hearts, such a call unsubstantiated by the logic of facts would be a dangerous foundation on which to build one's life, and more so when it meant test and trial for other men. But Christ did command his disciples to be witnesses for him "unto the uttermost part of the earth," and simple obedience to this plain command has justified itself in history. In spite of all parallelisms in the spiritual experi-ence of men of different faiths, the testimony of so many who in spite of ardent and ceaseless search did not and could not find their hearts' desire anywhere except in Jesus, must carry weight as an argument in itself. The fact that the spiritual genius of any man is adequate to the apprehension of God in Christ, is an an-swer by itself to the question, "Is Christ unique?"

And yet it is not enough of an answer to be sufficient as a basis for an evangelism which thinks of "the world for Christ." *Any* man can apprehend God in Christ. Yes, but must also *every* man? Is Christ unique?

The fourth answer to our question is an answer in terms of Christ's uniqueness. It is that *Christ must be exalted Lord, because of all the teachers and founders of religions he is the greatest, the noblest, the only sinless and true.*

He is, certainly, but only as judged by his own standards, and not if judged, for instance, by the standards of the Gita or of San-kara or of Buddha. He did no "nishkamya Karma"—unattached service; His works were shot through and through with purposive love. He asserted no identity with the being of all being; He lived claiming unity with God whom he called Father, and maintaining an attitude of piety toward Him which to us seems so human, and yet transcends all human piety in the clear assurance of God which was its fruit. He taught no absolute solution to the problem of suffering nor did he tell men how to escape it. He merely bore it himself, sharing our sin and sorrow, adding to the problem of the suffering of man the deeper problem of the suffering of God, and calling men not so much to escape a life so riddled with suffering, as to seek in him the strength and the hope to overcome suffering and use it for the building of a bigger life.

No, Christ is not the greatest among founders of religions except according to his own standards, and how shall we assert it of him when an absolute object standard outside the various religions does not exist? Along this line of reasoning the uniqueness of Christ cannot be proved at all.

When, however, we turn from these answers to look at the way in which the first apostles presented Christ, we find that their method was built on an altogether different approach to the question of Christ's uniqueness. They never argued about it. They lived and spoke as men who believed in it, and it was the quality of their commitment which convinced others. There was an urgency about their evangelism, an abandon about their faith and an otherworldliness about their life which bore uncompromising witness to Jesus as Lord. We shall never convince others about that which we do not take seriously ourselves, and it is precisely in taking Jesus seriously that we make clear his uniqueness. For it is not a uniqueness which we concede to him; it is rather a uniqueness with which he confronts us.

"The times of ignorance God overlooked, but now he commands all men everywhere to repent, because he has fixed a day on which he will judge the world in righteousness by a man whom he has appointed, and of this he has given assurance to all men by raising him from the dead" (Acts 17:30-31). In these words of St. Paul we see how the gap in the argument is filled. Jesus is announced Lord because Jesus has happened.

The uniqueness of Christ is a declared uniqueness

—declared with grace and truth in the life he lived and the death he died;

—declared with power by his resurrection from the dead and his living presence now;

—declared with contemporary significance by and in the
Church which is his body;

—declared as a self-validating fact by his ability to make himself God to men;

—declared as promise and as judgment when he said he would
come again in glory at the close of the age.

This uniqueness of Christ, therefore, which is declared by God
to faith cannot be a conviction to which men are led by any natural
transition of thought. It is rather a fact with which men are challenged and which establishes itself by the revolution it effects.
Jesus is the fulfiller rather than the fulfillment. He fulfills by sub-
stituting a new basis for values and lordship. He is not the coping
of a wall already raised. In Christ all things are brought under
one head, that by him as Lord, all things may be judged. To speak
in terms of Hinduism, the Gospel is not and cannot be the crown
of Hinduism. Hinduism does not point to him. But let a Hindu
be disturbed by being brought into contact with Christ and Christian influence, and then only Christ can fulfill the yearnings of
his soul.

The contact which the Gospel establishes, is established by
speaking into the situation rather than by speaking out of it; the
questions immanent in the situation being used to ask the real
question, What think ye of the Christ?

The reasons for evangelism may, therefore, be restated thus:

We preach Christ not because we have something to share
which he has done for us; but because he is the Christ who came
to do for all men all things that they need.

We preach Christ not because he alone can satisfy the spiritual longings of the human heart; but because, being Christ, he
alone ought to be the heart's deepest longing.

We preach Christ not because he has commanded us to
preach the Gospel to all the nations; but because he who has
so commanded has been declared to be the Christ.

We preach Christ not because of all the teachers and founders of all religions he is the greatest; but because he is himself the object of religion, dependably and unequivocally, God's Word to man.

Such is the faith that supports evangelism, and so is the Christ proclaimed. God grant that we may strive to this end, remembering that if we refuse or fail, then Christ must be crucified afresh; and it will be the lot of some other generation to witness to his inevitable Resurrection.

EPILOGUE

God called unto Moses and said: "Come now, therefore, and I will send thee unto Pharaoh, that thou mayest bring forth my people the children of Israel out of Egypt."

And Moses said unto God, "Who am I, that I should go unto Pharaoh?" Ex. 3:10-11

God has called me, but who am I?

Moses could boast of his royal upbringing, of his proficiency in the ancient learning of Egypt, of armies he had led to war, of battles he had won for the king; he could boast also of his passion for his own people, of his burning sense of justice which had set his hand against the hand of authority and had led him into the wilderness—and yet the word he speaks is a word of humiliation, the confession he makes is one of bankruptcy.

Why? He was standing before a bush that was burning without being consumed, and as he saw by it God's inexhaustible resources he saw also his own resourcelessness; while to his self-relevation there was added the sting of the task to which God bade him, a bidding that broke his nature wide open and showed him his own poverty.

We too must begin at our place of self-relevation, and for us that place is the cross. It was there that we saw God's inexhaustible resources—His love poured out without being emptied—and it was there that we lost the illusions about ourselves. We began there the life we live today, there we died and were born again, and still it is as we return there that we see ourselves most clearly.

We are not what others think we are. We are not what we have

115

been able to do or to achieve. We are not even what we have become in our striving after goodness. At the foot of the cross we all simply fall into one category—sinners.

Who am I that I should go unto Pharaoh. . . ? I am one sinner for whom Jesus died. This is the inner situation which is effected by and to which is addressed the call of God. "I will send thee unto Pharaoh."

Pharaoh knows Moses. He knows him as the man who grew up in his palace, and whom he has now dispossessed. Pharaoh knows the people of Israel. He knows them as the people whom he tried to destroy, and to whom now he has given the task of making bricks without straw. Pharaoh knows his own heart. He knows that he has deliberately hardened it, but he knows also that it was a hardening he could not help.

How true a picture of the world. It is to this world that we are sent! It is a world where the Christian faith is dispossessed of its hold on the mores of the people. It is a world that has sought to destroy the Church, and now has set the Church the task of building peace without providing it with the material either of repentance or of faith. It is a world that refuses to listen to God's Word and yet is also unable to listen or to understand. The Word of God itself has hardened the heart and made the ear heavy. And what is more, in the lands of the great religions, Pharaoh will not allow the people whom God calls to go forth and sacrifice to the Lord their God.

But is it to Pharaoh that Moses is sent? Is he not sent rather to the people themselves, to persuade them in the Name of God to accept God's Word to them; while it is God Himself who will deal with Pharaoh. "I will put forth my hand, and smite Egypt with all my wonders which I will do in the midst thereof: and after that he will let you go. . . . And when ye go, ye shall not go empty" (Ex. 3:20-21).

"The world is in the power of the evil one" (I John 5:19). We announce to it God's great demand, but it is God Himself who must and will deal with the demons of our time. And where the people obey and march forth at God's behest, Pharaoh's armies cannot follow. The people of God stand ranged on another front, and the Red Sea rolls between.

Precisely here, however, lies the source of our anguish. We must return again in conscious remembrance and renewal to the place of our decisive encounter with God. We must see ourselves as weaklings who go to Pharaoh in the strength of God's promise and His might. But will God act? Will He act in our time? Is the fall of Pharaoh near? "Lord, will you at this time restore the kingdom to Israel?" (Acts 1:6).

Those first disciples had been with Jesus for three crowded years. They had shared with hope in his proclamation of the Kingdom, they had watched with dismay his crucifixion and death. And then when all seemed lost Jesus had come back again. They saw him in power, the power that had conquered death. Their hopes had swelled high and ebbed low; but now seemed to be the time of fulfillment. . . . "Lord, is it now?"

We are very much in the same mood today. Our world seemed to be set for steady progress. The Church was full of the stories of triumphs in many lands. And then in one war after another Christendom broke to pieces and hopes lay shattered. Today, even after the noise of the guns has ceased—and it has not ceased yet in many lands—chaos remains. Those, however, whose eyes scan the far horizons speak of the glow of a coming day. But when?

The churches went through a great deal during the war. Some were lost for years in the silence but did not lose their faith. Some were tested by fire but were not found unfaithful. Some were challenged by the need of their sister churches and proved to be not unmindful. They all witness to their experience of the power of the risen Christ, and ask the question that lies nearest to their hearts, "Lord, is it now? When is the hour of fulfillment?"

Christ's answer to us is the same as his answer to those disciples of old: "It is not for you to know times or seasons which the Father has fixed by his own authority. But you shall receive power when the Holy Spirit has come upon you; and you shall be my witnesses in Jerusalem and in all Judea and Samaria and to the end of the earth" (Acts 1:7-8). That is your task, the rest is Mine.

Remember, however, that it is no new task which I give you, I send you in My Name, and you will go in the strength that springs from God's continuation in you and through you of what I have begun. The power you will show is the power of the leaven which I have already hid, the harvest you will reap is the harvest of the seed which I have already sown. The passions you will rouse are the passions of the fire which I have already kindled, the love you will share is the love of the deed which I have already done, and the end you will proclaim is the end of the end which I have already accomplished. Henceforth, the Son of man sits at the right hand of power, and shall come on the clouds of heaven.

Therefore shall ye be My witnesses:

—witnesses, as those who are able to discern the doings of God in a world where the doings of man are so obtrusive;
—witnesses, as those who point to the wonderful working of God, and claim for it the attention of their fellowmen;
—witnesses, as those who dare to quote themselves as part of the evidence of what God has wrought.

But even so the poignancy of the original question remains, and remains especially for us who are the young people of this generation. The future is our inheritance, and while we do not ask when the final consummation will be, we do seek to know the immediate prospect. To what end is our witnessing? Are we bidden to bear our witness "until cities be waste without inhabitant, and houses without man," and until only the stock remains which is the holy seed (Is. 6:11-13), or are we bidden to bear our witness until men "turn every one from his evil way, and from the violence that is in his hands" and God too turns again and forgives them (Jonah 3:8-10)? Do we stand as before Jerusalem or as before Nineveh?

The answer to these questions is part of the witness we must bring, and will condition also all our witnessing. But have we an answer? or only the possibility of many answers, all of which stem from the ultimate answer that God is God? Will it be peace or war? and what must Christians do about it? Many answers to this question are possible, but no answer is true which forgets that neither man nor nations nor churches can organize an escape from the consequences of sin except it be by way of repentance and amendment of life. God is God, and there is no other God. *"I am that I am* is My name. Go, therefore, and I shall be with thy mouth, and teach thee what thou shalt speak."

Moses doubted the sufficiency of this answer to the questions he had raised, and he took to himself an Aaron to help him—Aaron who later helped the people to worship the golden calf. No, God's answer is sufficient, and it is sufficient only when it stands alone sustaining faith and undergirding obedience. It is natural to cry, "Oh that I knew where I might find him! That I might come even to his seat! when he doth work" (Job 23:3, 9). And yet it is enough to be able to say, "But he knoweth the way that I take" (Job 23:10).

Thus are we able to bear our witness to Him:

—witnessing in Jerusalem, among those who know us best, whether in church or office or home, and where the witness of life counts most;
—witnessing in Judea, among those whose loyalty to the past hinders their obedience in the present;
—witnessing in Samaria, among those between whom and us the years have erected walls of mistrust and bitterness;
—and witnessing unto the uttermost part of the earth.

For the Christian witness recognizes no barrier and allows no partiality. We are witnesses to the colored peoples and to the white. We are witnesses within the Western nations as well as in the Eastern. We are witnesses among peoples of all religions and no religion. We are witnesses among the outcast, the refugee, the displaced person . . . witnesses unto the uttermost part of the earth.

So do we prove the fullness of His promise, "Lo, I am with you alway even unto the end of the world": alway and all the way, unto earth's remotest end and until the end, when shall be established "SALVATION AND POWER; THE KINGDOM OF OUR GOD AND THE AUTHORITY OF HIS CHRIST."

GLOSSARY

Anatta   Soul-less-ness; absence of self.

Anicca   Impermanence; transitoriness.

Atta   Soul; self.

Dhamma   Law; doctrine; right.

Didache   The teaching about the Gospel given to new members of the early Christian Church.

Dukkha   Sorrow; care.

Evangel   The Gospel.

Existentialism   A philosophical theory, stressing the individual's responsibility for making himself what he is.

Kamma   Result of action; chain of causation.

Kenosis   An act of emptying (Phil. 2:7).

Kerygma   The proclamation by early Christians of the Gospel to non-Christians.

Nibbana   Emancipation; state of release.

Nicca   Eternal; permanent; timeless.

Nishkamya Karma   This is a conception in the Bhagavad Gita. The literal meaning of the word is "desireless works." The idea is that service must be rendered without any sense of attachment either to the service itself as a life purpose, or to the person served, or to any possible reward of service. The nearest Western conception is that of Kant—"duty for duty's sake."

Shaliach   Messenger.